"All of Gordon Fee's students, colleagues, fr[...] heart and tears. His profound love for Jesus [...] versations, prayers—and in this book. Fee also writes [...] friend Paul and presents the Apostle's devotion to Christ with crisp clarity and accessible language. *Jesus the Lord according to Paul the Apostle* is likely Gordon's last work, written for the church and students he loved. Read the words, know the heart, and come to love Jesus Christ with wonder and joy."

—**Gene L. Green**, Wheaton College and Graduate School

"One of the signal biblical scholars of our day, Gordon Fee has scaled down his magisterial *Pauline Christology* into a more modest size to be accessible to serious students and busy clergy. The immense scope of Fee's learning is still evident in this edition, but here is a four-part synthesis of the most important and constructive themes of Paul's witness to the risen Christ. Especially important is Fee's well-regarded defense of Paul's incarnational Christology and its strategic role in his messianic conception of God's salvation. Readers of Scripture will appreciate Fee's discussion of Paul's running dialogue with his Bible, the Greek translation of the synagogue's Hebrew Scripture, to lend biblical support to his core theological claim that Messiah Jesus is God's Son. Fee records Paul's dynamic struggle of relating his new belief in a divine Jesus to his own Judaism's monotheism. An excellent resource for the seminary classroom and parish library."

—**Robert W. Wall**, Seattle Pacific University and Seminary

"I cut my intellectual teeth on Gordon Fee's 1 Corinthians commentary as an undergraduate student. Again and again his academic insight astounded me, and his pastoral wisdom and overt Pentecostal spirituality encouraged me. Almost twenty years later my respect for him has not diminished; I routinely check his works in my own research and teaching. So many of his areas of scholarly and practical passion combine in *Jesus the Lord according to Paul the Apostle*, including his careful reading of texts, his emphasis on Christian behavior (as opposed to 'works'), his interest in the Spirit, and his bridge work between biblical studies and systematic theology. This is a classic Fee feast. Chew on this. Chew well."

—**Holly Beers**, Westmont College

JESUS

the LORD according to

PAUL

the APOSTLE

JESUS
the LORD according to
PAUL
the APOSTLE

A CONCISE INTRODUCTION

GORDON D. FEE

Foreword by Cherith Fee Nordling

Baker Academic
a division of Baker Publishing Group
Grand Rapids, Michigan

Published by Baker Academic
a division of Baker Publishing Group
PO Box 6287, Grand Rapids, MI 49516-6287
www.bakeracademic.com

Printed in the United States of America

Portions of this book are adapted from *Pauline Christology*, Baker Academic, 2007.

Library of Congress Cataloging-in-Publication Data
Names: Fee, Gordon D., author.
Title: Jesus the Lord according to Paul the Apostle : a concise introduction / Gordon D. Fee.
Description: Grand Rapids : Baker Academic, 2018. | Includes index.
Identifiers: LCCN 2017028399 | ISBN 9780801049828 (pbk. : alk. paper)
Subjects: LCSH: Jesus Christ—Person and offices. | Bible. Epistles of Paul—Theology.
Classification: LCC BT205 .F36 2018 | DDC 232—dc23
LC record available at https://lccn.loc.gov/2017028399

18 19 20 21 22 23 24   7 6 5 4 3 2 1

Contents

Part 4 The Jewish Messiah and Exalted Lord 117

Foreword

The idea for this book was born on a sun-dappled day as my father and I sat together on our deck on Galiano Island, British Columbia, reviewing pages for his soon-to-be-published *Pauline Christology*. The dry day held a gentle breeze. Water lapped on the rocks below us. There were sounds of a boat's sail snapping as it passed, the snort of a seal fishing below the deck, and the occasional whoops and laughter of kids jumping from the nearby tree swing. And in the midst of it all, warmth and enthusiasm radiated from my father as we read the page proofs together. They beautifully and rigorously described Paul's understanding of and relation to the person of Jesus of Nazareth, Son of God, Lord and Christ. As we worked that afternoon, I realized again how deeply and similarly Paul and my father loved Jesus. And once more, as had happened so many times when reading through the lens of Paul alongside my father, something moved from knowledge to understanding, from understanding to wisdom, from knowing *about* to *relational* knowing. Paul and my father had again drawn me into deeper knowledge of and more profound love for Jesus.

That summer day I secretly hoped that the summary chapters we were reading from *Pauline Christology* would one day be accessible to the wider church and that it would offer as much life and joy as my father's other smaller summary book on Paul's understanding of and relation to the Holy Spirit, *Paul, the Spirit, and the People of God*. And here it is! This book is another gift to thoughtful believers who want to know Jesus and his whole life in relation to their own human lives, meaningfully renewed in his image. Moreover, this is most likely the last book that my father will publish in his long career. This realization, coupled with the deeply transformative impact this material has had on my own life and work and that of my students, has led me to write this personal foreword gratefully and unapologetically.

. In the larger *Pauline Christology*, and now in these pages, we meet the very same, still incarnate Lord who encountered Saul of Tarsus two thousand years ago while Saul was transporting deadly warrants for Damascene Christians. When that brilliant Jewish scholar, Pharisee, and zealot met the Lord, Yahweh himself, in the resurrected flesh of Jesus, accompanied by the blinding, healing power of the Holy Spirit, everything he understood in relation to God and the world was upended and reoriented, undeniably and forever. God's embodied grace, love, and righteousness were made radically self-evident in the revelation of his Son, and this cruciform love transformed Saul of Tarsus into Paul, apostle of the Lord, Jesus Christ. God's grace in Christ, which had reordered the world's *telos*, or goal, now reordered Paul's world, transforming his identity and calling to a new, predominantly gentile people for God's name. His devotion to Yahweh and his recognition of God's purposes from first creation through new creation took on a trinitarian cast—to the one Holy Spirit, the one Lord Jesus, and the one God and Father of all.

Over the years, Paul became a dear friend of my dad, who had also experienced the love and grace of our risen Lord and a subsequent call to bear witness to him. My father first introduced me to his friend Paul when I was young. As an early teen I found Paul rough, unpredictable in tone, and sometimes a little arrogant—for example, when he appealed to the Thessalonian church to imitate him. One evening while in junior high, I confessed to my father that I wasn't sure I liked Paul. That night he sat with me in his basement study and asked me what I heard in Paul's words and what images and feelings they brought up in me. He also shared with me a bit of Paul's perspective. He told me backstories about these churches and Paul and the relationships between them. As we talked, I realized that my ambivalence revealed my small, rather legalistic gospel and its concomitant nagging shame.

My father's questions, however, also revealed in me a longing for Paul's fearless love of God and his joy of being loved by God. I recognized this same fearless love in my father, and I realized then that my dad knew and loved Jesus much like he knew and loved Paul. Moreover, my father knew and loved Paul with empathy, gratitude, and respect. And most of all, he trusted Paul's experience of God. If Paul was unapproachable and at times unassailably holy to me, he was not so to my father. My father helped me realize that Paul's call for the Thessalonian community to imitate him was rooted in a shared love for and trust in the Lord and one another. I began to consider that some people addressed in Paul's letters would hear him differently because they knew him so much better than I did. And some, like me, would hear him with ambivalence because they didn't yet know and trust God—or Paul—like my father and others did. Yet for all of us, trusting and ambivalent alike, Paul's words occasioned experiences of God's gracious renewal in our lives, through his consistent message of God's lavish, costly love in and through his Son and the nonnegotiable life of God's people by the Holy Spirit.

Over the next few years, my father continued to invite me into shared conversations with him and Paul, and Paul became more approachable as I got to know him better. Both Paul and my dad were deeply moved by God's love, and I too wanted to know God that way. Since that evening in the study, as my life in Christ by the Spirit grew richer and more challenging, Paul and his churches became more real to me, and my curiosity grew. I was intrigued by the way Paul embedded Jesus's story and theirs in Old Testament stories and metaphors that he seemed to take for granted but that I didn't understand at all. Typical high schooler, I wanted the background drama and the dirt: What led to Paul's expressions of pastoral love, concern, frustration, joy, warning, celebration, scolding, and delight in these relationships, both assumed and named? In my finer moments, I wanted to understand better the context for this grand story of God and the world made known in the crucified Lord and to see it unfold in the lives of the New Testament communities so that I could better recognize this story unfolding in my own life and community.

My high school years in New England included belonging to a house church that met on our living room floor. Weekly we sang, shared, prayed, cried, laughed, and ate together. And I watched my father regularly well up in tears of wonder and love at the grace of God in Christ, often expressed through Paul's love for Christ permeating that space as my dad would share from one of Paul's epistles. My dad's tears were not unique to our living room floor, however. I heard students in that gathering talk of how my dad couldn't make it through a lecture without tearing up. And then, early one November evening after my shift ended at work, I stopped by the seminary to pick up my dad on the way home. His office was the only one lit up, and I headed into the building to get him. The office door was open, but I didn't see him inside. Then I heard a muffled sound. Walking around the side of his desk, I found him on the floor, in tears. "Dad, are you OK?" "Sure am, honey," he said, as he sniffled, got up, and blew his nose. "I was just preparing the lecture for class tomorrow. The gospel never ceases to amaze me." Looking at his desk, I saw his Greek outline of one of Paul's epistles for an advanced exegesis class. Not everyone's devotional cup of tea, I grant you! But for my dad, who was spending time again with Paul, immersed in the lavish good news of God in Christ by the Spirit, this was familiar worship space. I had interrupted him there, on the floor, held in the love of the Triune God.

It is no wonder that during the winter months ahead, I voluntarily sat in a room full of church folk I didn't know, listening to my father teach a New Testament survey course. My personal hungers for God and for a less individualistic reading of the Scriptures grew together. And Paul's costly devotion to Jesus was always before me. When I was tempted to go off the rails at the end of high school, it was precisely because of the costliness of the gospel in my own life in regard to my friendships. My parents eventually called me back home in the most Pauline of ways, reminding me that our family belonged to each other, that we needed each other to be who we were made to be, and that without one another—shaped and held together in trust and unconditional love—we couldn't become who we were meant to be.

By the time I went off to college, my dad's friend Paul had become my grown-up friend. In Paul's letters I heard Jesus—and my dad—calling me to the grand realities of the gospel in the new relationships given to me, and I grew into greater conformity to Christ, individually and communally. Uniquely, Robert and I heard Jesus's voice ringing through both my dad's and Paul's voices at our wedding, when my dad drew on Paul's words to call us to our shared life and union with the Triune God. I hope that my own voice echoed theirs when months later, fresh out of college, I led a group of women twice my age in a study of Paul's letter to the church at Philippi. That experience brought a whole new level of trust as we wrestled through life together under the transformative power of Jesus offered to us by our brother Paul: receiving his offering of life in the Spirit to the praise of our Father in heaven; recognizing that Paul not only was familiar with pain and hardship but also assumed that this was part of the reality of being joined to Christ; and seeing with Paul that Christ had joined himself to us and our pain in order to speak a different, glorious final word over our lives.

It has been a joy and privilege as an adult to continue to walk alongside my father, to eavesdrop on his academic work, and to witness the transformative power of that work in each of our lives and communities and in the lives and communities of countless others. My dad's work on his Corinthians commentary flowed into my reading, prayer, and meditation, offering insight into my church community in California as we learned more about life in the Spirit. I remember similar conversations during my dad's work on his Philippians commentary as it impacted both his church and his community at Regent College. It was this deep recognition of the interrelationship between his academic work and the life of the church that led him and my mom to embark on the labor of love of turning the nearly one-thousand-page *God's Empowering Presence* into *Paul, the Spirit, and the People of God*—a shorter tour of the same material that would be affordable and manageable for a wider audience of brothers and sisters deeply in need of Paul's wisdom in their lives and the lives of their communities.

As I pursued my own doctoral work in systematic theology over the next decade, I returned again and again to these texts and to my father's reflections on Paul's writings in real time to real churches in particular situations. The systematic theology I read in my studies generally attempted to order belief about God into a coherent whole. But we don't find Paul doing theology like this in his letters. He doesn't reflect systematically on the person and work of Christ Jesus, or on that of the Holy Spirit, or on the Triune persons in relation, though all of these are presupposed and surface in focused ways, especially in his prayers. Rather, Paul's letters emerge from the particular relationships he has with God's new people. He speaks to the unique concerns of these churches in light of their identity as God's children by the Spirit and the impact of the gospel on their communal relationships and in their broader cultural contexts as people living God's future kingdom life in the present. As I began teaching undergraduates and mentoring student leaders, *Paul, the Spirit, and the People of God* was an invaluable aid. The particularity of Paul's efforts to teach communal life in the Spirit to his New Testament communities helped the students I was teaching to glimpse life in the Spirit in their own contexts. Again and again, I was grateful that my parents had undertaken the journey of turning my dad's academic work into an accessible resource for the church. Through that book, Paul's words to the early church were helping transform twenty-first-century lives in the power of the Holy Spirit.

A similar transformation began to work its way through me that afternoon on Galiano Island as my father and I reviewed the page proofs for *Pauline Christology*. In Paul's letters, we hear him reflecting, provoking, rejoicing, wooing, criticizing, encouraging, blessing, and calling forward the church as God's new people, saved *from* sin and death and saved *for* renewed life as God's immortal human children made to rule over a new creation. Paul does so because he has met the world's new Adam, the firstborn from among the dead, whose life they share as coheirs with Christ by the resurrecting Spirit of adoption, who will bring to completion their glorious, eternal human life. With Paul, we discover the person of Jesus Christ as the self-revelation of God's triune life and purposes. Those purposes, in Paul's words, have been intended and moved forward from before creation to their climax in Christ and are now moving toward their ultimate, unstoppable beginning, held in Jesus until his final advent.

While much is written on Paul's soteriology, too often these studies sidestep Paul's understanding of and love for the person of Jesus of Nazareth, the Son of God. Paul does not separate Christ's person from his work. Systematic theology may try, but to do so is to fail to account for the fact that the person implies the work and vice versa. Both Christ's person and his work are firmly embedded in Israel's history. Jesus's title

Kyrios (Lord) emerges from the language of LORD in the Greek Old Testament; Paul presents Jesus as Israel's Messiah, or anointed one (Christ). Yet Paul grasps that through the climax of Israel's history in Christ Jesus, God has opened the future story of the entire cosmos.

As I read *Pauline Christology* with my dad that afternoon, I marveled in a new way at Jesus's humanity in particular. What struck me was the off-handed way that Jesus's humanity was taken for granted by Paul and by my father as Paul's companion. Sometimes our theology sidesteps Christ's humanity in making the case for his divinity so that we forget that Christ as the resurrected new Adam is not a metaphor but the primary reality and hope on which our present and future human life rests. For Paul there was nothing metaphorical about it. If Paul rarely brings aspects of Jesus's daily human life to the fore, it is because he takes the humanness of that life for granted. Jesus's authentic humanity did not surprise him, apart from Jesus's astonishing alignment with and sinless obedience to the Father by the power of the Spirit. "Why didn't Paul remind us of Jesus's human life by the Spirit more often?" I wondered aloud as I worked alongside my father. "Why would he think he had to?" my father asked me quizzically. The radicalism of Paul's Christology is not his emphasis on Jesus's humanity but his equation of Jesus with God: God Incarnate among us but not using that to his advantage (hence living submitted to the Spirit), crucified and resurrected, now exalted and reigning, and bringing God's Spirit-born children into the first stages of their new eschatological life together.

In the years since, this renewed understanding of Jesus's humanity, glimpsed in the pages of *Pauline Christology*, has permeated my Christian understanding as well as my academic writing and teaching. Just as I relied on *Paul, the Spirit, and the People of God* in my early years of teaching and mentoring students in life in the Spirit, so too I have come to rely on the material in this book as I teach and mentor students regarding Jesus's resurrected and ascended humanity and the promises therein for our own renewed humanity. Jesus's ongoing, glorified humanity is such good news for the church. Yet without a shorter, more accessible version of the material in *Pauline Christology*, it remains out of reach for many. I have hoped for many years that this material would be made accessible for the broader church, the way my parents developed *Paul, the Spirit, and the People of God* from the material in *God's Empowering Presence.* I am delighted that *Jesus the Lord according to Paul the Apostle* finally fulfills that hope.

Over the years, one of my great joys has been meeting others who have been similarly transformed by my father's writing and teaching on Paul. "His love for Jesus, the Father, and the Spirit, changed my life." "I've been drawn into the triune life and love of God by this man whose whole life has been committed and held therein." "I didn't know life in the Spirit until I heard the invitation through him." So often fellow academics, sisters and brothers in the church, students, and seminarians have told me these things—sometimes about Paul and sometimes about my father. My dad has spent so much time in Paul's company— this friend from among the great cloud of witnesses, his brother, soul mate, and coheir within the communion of the saints. And Paul has led my father over and over again to their shared Lord and elder brother, into whose image they both are being transformed. Paul's remarkable experience of being set free from legalism through an encounter with the divine Christ and his ministry in response to that relationship and calling have continued to draw my father—and through him, me and so many others—into deeper relationship with and transformation into the image of our ascended brother and Lord. If this is my father's last work, what better way could there be to finish?

Cherith Fee Nordling
Associate Professor of Theology
Northern Seminary, Lisle, Illinois

Preface

I n the course of a longtime interest in all things Pauline in the New Testament, I became aware of two considerable gaps in the scholarly literature that seemed worth pursuing: Paul's understanding of the Holy Spirit and his understanding of the person of Christ. Since my personal concerns have always been with a biblical theology that flowed directly out of a careful analysis of the data, the two books that emerged out of those concerns, *God's Empowering Presence* and *Pauline Christology*, ended up at a somewhat forbidding length.[1] I have long been concerned about books on biblical theology that give the reader only the final results of an author's exegesis of the biblical texts without offering a look at how the author came to those conclusions. That concern played itself out in two very heavy tomes (what a *New York Times* reviewer of such a book once described as "big enough to kill a cockroach in a shag rug"!). But since the ultimate driving force of both projects was to make the results more accessible to any interested reader of Scripture, I decided to cull the theological material from both books and present it in a more accessible format, resulting in what one of my children regularly refers to as my "small Paul" books.

1. *God's Empowering Presence: The Holy Spirit in the Letters of Paul* (Grand Rapids: Baker Academic, 2011 [Peabody, MA: Hendrickson, 1994]) came to 992 pages, while *Pauline Christology: An Exegetical-Theological Study* (Grand Rapids: Baker Academic, 2007 [Peabody, MA: Hendrickson, 2007]) came to 740 pages.

The first "small Paul" book, published as *Paul, the Spirit, and the People of God*,[2] presents Paul's doctrine of the Holy Spirit in a more accessible way than the longer *God's Empowering Presence*. Likewise, the present book presents the theological synthesis of my exegetical work on Paul's Christology in a way that might be more accessible to a wider readership than the larger *Pauline Christology*.

The present volume is divided into four parts. Part 1 describes Christ as Savior by offering an overview of what salvation in Christ meant for the Apostle and then examining the christological implications of Paul's thoroughly christocentric worldview, especially as it emerges in his Christ devotion. That leads to an examination of Paul's understanding of Christ as preexistent, since it is otherwise nearly impossible to account for such Christ devotion by an avid monotheist unless his understanding of the one God now included the Son of God in the divine identity.

Preexistence as God also means that the Jesus of history must be understood in terms of an incarnation, and such an understanding by Paul must be taken seriously: the divine Son of God lived a truly human life on our planet. So part 2 picks up the question of Christ's humanity by way of Paul's use of "Adam" and the crucial word *eikōn* ("image") from Genesis 1–2, pointing out that the ultimate concern in this analogy is emphasis both on Christ's genuine humanity and on his bearing and restoring the divine image lost in the fall.

Parts 3 and 4 pursue the two primary christological emphases that emerge regularly in the corpus and that arguably hold the keys to Paul's answer to the question of who Christ is. The suggested answer is that Christ is, first of all, the Jewish Messiah and Son of God (part 3), and second, the now exalted "lord" of Psalm 110:1 (part 4), who for Paul has come to be identified with *Kyrios* (= Yahweh), which was how the Septuagint handled the divine name. Since this exclusive usage of "Lord" for Christ tends to dominate Paul's understanding of Christ in his present kingly reign, I conclude not only with a rehearsal of the many ways that Paul refers to Christ by way of presupposition, attributing to him activities that a monotheistic Jew would attribute to God alone, but also by considering how Paul perceives the relationship of the Son to the Father, since he

2. Grand Rapids: Baker Academic, 2011 (Peabody, MA: Hendrickson, 1996).

never abandons—indeed, he stoutly retains—his historic monotheism. On the one hand, there are those several texts where it appears certain that Paul understands Christ in terms of eternal divinity; on the other hand, and whatever else, there are not thereby two divinities. So in the end, larger theological questions regarding the Trinity must be raised.

A few observations about the present volume are in order. First, readers will notice that the four parts are not even close to being of equal length. This disparity is not intentional but is the result of my attempt to present each aspect of Paul's Christology in its own part. And since some aspects of Paul's Christology simply require more headings—each of which I have treated in a separate chapter—some unevenness inevitably results.

Second, readers familiar with *Pauline Christology* will notice that the present book omits not only the large first part of that volume, which offers my detailed exegetical analysis of each of Paul's letters, but also the two appendixes there, including the considerable appendix on "Christ and Personified Wisdom." As I discuss in that appendix, I believe that so-called wisdom Christology was one of the more misguided moments in the history of New Testament scholarship. In my view, wisdom Christology has not an exegetical leg of any kind on which to stand, and fortunately it seems to be waning in Pauline scholarship. In the language of Tennyson, this little system had its day and has now ceased to be. As Paul makes clear in his scathing demolition of the alleged wisdom of the believers in Corinth (1 Cor. 1:18–2:5), the only "wisdom" Paul knew or cared about was what he very deliberately called "God's foolishness," having to do with salvation through the ultimate oxymoron of a "crucified Messiah." God, Paul insists, has chosen to do away with human wisdom by way of this ultimate "divine folly." Only the eternal God is so "wise" as to demolish human pride in such an unimaginable way. As the gospel songwriter Edward Mote put it nearly two centuries ago, our hope is built on nothing less than Jesus's *blood* and righteousness. Our faith rests altogether on the crucifixion and resurrection of the incarnate one, the one who chose to enter our impoverished human existence and lived and died so that through the risen one we might have true life in the present and eternal life with the redeemer and his redeemed.

Third, as in all academic disciplines, New Testament scholarship has its own set of technical terms that are not always shared by readers outside the discipline. I have therefore included a glossary of technical terms for the sake of nonspecialist readers, in hopes that it will somewhat alleviate what for some could easily become burdensome reading.

Finally, unless noted otherwise, all renderings of the Bible into English are taken from the New International Version (2011), on whose committee I have served with great pleasure since 1988. Aside from adding italics on occasion for emphasis or to highlight various features of the text, there is one point in which I alter this translation—namely, by inserting a comma between "Lord" and "Jesus Christ" in order to distinguish the "title" from the "name," as I explain in part 4. I have chosen for convenience to present the biblical text at the outset of each discussion and without the verse numbers, which have their way of obstructing good reading. Fully aware that presenting the biblical text will get in the way of some people's normal reading, I nevertheless thought that making it easier for readers to review the biblical text when I refer to specific passages would be better than forcing them to break up their reading by consulting the Bible on their own at each point. Still I believe it would benefit those who choose—as I could only wish they would—to be as the Berean Jews who "examined the Scriptures every day to see if what Paul said was true" (Acts 17:11). In this case, of course, their examination will help them to determine the truth of the interpretation of Paul set forth in this study!

Gordon D. Fee

Abbreviations

General

=	equals	e.g.	exempli gratia (for example)
//	parallel passage	Gk.	Greek
ca.	circa (around)	i.e.	id est (that is)
CE	Common Era	lit.	literally
cf.	confer (compare)	trans.	translation
chap(s).	chapter(s)	v(v).	verse(s)

Bible Versions

ESV	English Standard Version	NIV	New International Version
KJV	King James Version	NLT	New Living Translation
LXX	Septuagint (Greek Old Testament)	NRSV	New Revised Standard Version
NAB	New American Bible		

Old Testament

Gen.	Genesis	1–2 Chron.	1–2 Chronicles
Exod.	Exodus	Ezra	Ezra
Lev.	Leviticus	Neh.	Nehemiah
Num.	Numbers	Esther	Esther
Deut.	Deuteronomy	Job	Job
Josh.	Joshua	Ps. (Pss.)	Psalms
Judg.	Judges	Prov.	Proverbs
Ruth	Ruth	Eccles.	Ecclesiastes
1–2 Sam.	1–2 Samuel	Song	Song of Songs
1–2 Kings	1–2 Kings	Isa.	Isaiah

Jer.	Jeremiah	Jon.	Jonah
Lam.	Lamentation	Mic.	Micah
Ezek.	Ezekiel	Nah.	Nahum
Dan.	Daniel	Hab.	Habakkuk
Hosea	Hosea	Zeph.	Zephaniah
Joel	Joel	Hag.	Haggai
Amos	Amos	Zech.	Zechariah
Obad.	Obadiah	Mal.	Malachi

New Testament

Matt.	Matthew	1–2 Thess.	1–2 Thessalonians
Mark	Mark	1–2 Tim.	1–2 Timothy
Luke	Luke	Titus	Titus
John	John	Philem.	Philemon
Acts	Acts	Heb.	Hebrews
Rom.	Romans	James	James
1–2 Cor.	1–2 Corinthians	1–2 Pet.	1–2 Peter
Gal.	Galatians	1–3 John	1–3 John
Eph.	Ephesians	Jude	Jude
Phil.	Philippians	Rev.	Revelation
Col.	Colossians		

PART 1

The Savior

The primary goal of this study is to offer a careful analysis of the apostle Paul's understanding of the person of Christ, that is, *who* it was who came among us and *why* he did so. I argue that Christ came among us for two basic reasons: first, to reveal the true nature and character of the eternal God and, second, to redeem us from our fallen, and thus broken, condition. But to get to those conclusions it seems wise to begin where Paul himself began: with what Christ *did* for us through his incarnation, including his life, crucifixion, resurrection, and ascension. The reason for beginning here is that what Christ accomplished by revelation and redemption (his *work*) is based altogether on who he was and is (his *person*). His work and his person are so tied together in Paul's view that we can begin to understand his person by first examining his work. Parts 1 and 2, therefore, offer an overview of the Apostle's understanding of Christ's saving work—the doctrinal locus that theologians refer to as *soteriology*. Before turning in part 2 to Christ's work as creator of a new humanity, in part 1 we focus on his work as Savior of humanity by examining how Paul views Jesus as both the divine Savior (chap. 1) and the preexistent and incarnate Savior (chap. 2).

1

The Divine Savior

The phrase *salvation in Christ* may well serve as the basic summation of Paul's central concerns regarding both Christian experience and Christian theology. Paul unpacks his christological soteriology in four ways: through a consistent *grammar* of salvation; an *eschatological framework* for salvation; an identification of the people of God made in Christ's image as the *goal* of salvation; and an identification of the death and resurrection of Christ as the *means* of salvation.

First, Paul uses a rather consistent *grammar* of salvation, which takes the following triadic form: salvation is predicated on the love of God the Father, effected through the death and resurrection of Christ the Son, and made effective through the Spirit of God, who is also the Spirit of the Son. Thus in the earliest passage of its kind in his preserved letters, Paul identifies the believers in Thessalonica in the following way: "brothers and sisters loved by *the Lord* [= *Kyrios*],[1] because *God* chose you as firstfruits to be saved through the sanctifying work of *the Spirit*"

1. The Apostle uses the noun *Kyrios*—which our English Bibles regularly render "Lord"—to refer to Christ alone. This is remarkable since for several centuries before the coming of Christ, the Jewish community had used this "name" as their substitute for "Yahweh" so as never to take God's *name* in vain. One of the seldom noted reasons for the Jewish community's antipathy toward the followers of Jesus was the latter's consistent use of the substitute name for Yahweh, *Kyrios*, to refer only to the risen Jesus of Nazareth. For the Jewish community, this was the ultimate blasphemy, which caused such a devotee as Saul of Tarsus to persecute

3

(2 Thess. 2:13; ca. 49 CE). This threefold way of speaking about our salvation continues throughout his letters to the very end: "*God our Savior
. . .* saved us through the washing of rebirth and renewal by *the Holy
Spirit*, whom [*God*] poured out generously through *Jesus Christ our Savior*"
(Titus 3:4–7; ca. 65 CE). Indeed, this triadic way of speaking about salvation, which resulted from the earliest believers' experience of salvation,
is the primary New Testament basis for the eventual articulation of the
doctrine of the Trinity. It was formulated under Emperor Constantine
during the fourth century when he called for a church council to address
the issue of language about the Trinity. They drafted a document that
eventually became one of the creeds of the church.[2]

One might note, for example, Paul's rather off-the-cuff introduction to
his response to the Corinthian believers regarding Spirit-gifting: "There
are different kinds of gifts, but the same *Spirit* distributes them. There
are different kinds of service, but the same *Lord* [= *Kyrios*]. There are
different kinds of working, but in all of them and in everyone it is the
same *God* at work" (1 Cor. 12:1–3). Whatever language one uses for this
divine triadic phenomenon, which eventually was given the designation
of the Trinity, justice is done to Paul only when one recognizes that
human salvation is grounded in and accomplished by the one and only
God: Father, Son, and Holy Spirit.

Second, Paul's soteriology employs a thoroughly *eschatological framework*, meaning that Christ's death and resurrection and the gift of the
Spirit mark the turning of the ages. Indeed, the consistent worldview of
the several and varied writers of the documents that became our New
Testament was that, with the coming of Christ, God has set in motion

followers of Jesus vigorously so as to bring them to justice before God. Then Saul himself
became a disciple of Jesus and, after coming to use the name Paul, adopted this very practice.

2. In addition to leading to the development of trinitarian doctrine, the early church's triadic
formulation for salvation also likely fueled the Jewish community's sometimes hostile—
especially in the case of Saul of Tarsus—antipathy toward the early disciples of Jesus. Along
with the use of *Kyrios* for Jesus, this triadic formulation helps to explain Saul's driving hatred
of the nascent Christians, all of whom initially were Jews who had become disciples of Christ.
For Saul, Jesus's crucifixion served as the primary evidence that the one and only God had given
Jesus of Nazareth what he well deserved. But it was in God's own wisdom that the brilliant
and totally incensed Saul of Tarsus would—not by his own choice, to be sure—eventually be
chosen as the groundbreaker who, as Paul, would lead the nascent Christian faith to reach
out to the known world so as also to include gentiles.

the *new* creation, in which all things will eventually be made new at the eschatological conclusion of the present age.

Third, for Paul the ultimate *goal* of human redemption is not simply saving individuals and fitting them for heaven, as it were—and as true as that may be—but is rather the creation of a people for God's name, reconstituted by a new covenant.[3] Although people in the new covenant are saved one by one, the ultimate goal of that salvation is the formation of a people who in their life together—as with Israel of old—reflect the character of the God who redeemed them. After all, the biblical narrative begins with humans purposely created in the divine image. For Paul the true *eikōn*, or image, of the eternal God was borne by Christ in his incarnation, and Christ in turn is in the process of re-creating a new people of God in his image through the work of the Spirit.

Fourth, for Paul the *means* of salvation is Jesus of Nazareth's death on the cross and subsequent resurrection, which in turn was followed by the coming of the Holy Spirit to enable those of us who live in the present self-absorbed culture to live *Christianly* instead. Thus through what turned out to be the truly single great world-shaking event, the eternal God has chosen to redeem fallen humanity from their enslavement to self and sin so that death itself is thereby defeated. A careful reading of Paul reveals that all of his basic theological concerns are an outworking of his fundamental confession, found in one of his earliest letters that was written within two decades of the events themselves: "that Christ died for our sins according to the Scriptures, that he was buried, [and] that he was raised on the third day according to the Scriptures" (1 Cor. 15:3–4; cf. Rom. 4:25). In a way that lies beyond all merely human imagination, we are told that Jesus was delivered over to death as an atonement for our sins and was raised to life for our justification, or redemption.

Although the first of these foundational propositions reflects the ultimate concern of this study, in this chapter we focus on these last two points: how Christ serves as both the goal and the means of salvation. Special attention is paid to Christ as the goal of salvation since this idea

3. Incidentally, this is perhaps the element missing the most in American Christianity since the United States' national heritage has had a singular focus on the individual rather than on the gathered people as a community of faith who in our life together demonstrate the true nature of what it means to be saved.

is seldom brought forward in discussions of Paul's soteriology and since the role of Christ is not always as immediately obvious here as it is at other points.

The Goal of Salvation: Re-creation into the Divine Image

The People of God

One of the serious weaknesses of much traditional Protestant theology is its proclivity toward a doctrine of salvation (soteriology) devoid of a serious doctrine of the church (ecclesiology). That is, the tendency is to focus on salvation in an individualistic way that loses the "people of God" dimension of Paul's perspective. This is due in large part to a presuppositional emphasis, especially in much Protestant theology, on discontinuity between the two covenants, with very little appreciation for the significant dimension of continuity. This presuppositional emphasis fails to recognize that such individualism is very much the product of modern Western civilization and that it scarcely, if at all, existed in the first century.

To be sure, the beginning point of *dis*continuity resides in the significant reality that entrance into the people of God under the new covenant happens individually, one by one, through faith in Christ Jesus and the enabling of the Spirit. As with all the New Testament documents, Paul's letters in particular presuppose that they were written to first-generation believers who became so precisely in this way. Also of significance is that the churches to whom Paul is writing two decades into the Christian era were by then composed of more gentiles than Jews. How second-generation believers become members of the household of God is an area of huge debate and division among later Christians, in large part because these earliest believers could not have imagined that twenty centuries would follow them. The subsequent debate and division have happened in part because Paul, not to mention the rest of the New Testament, simply does not speak specifically to the matter of second-generation believers. Nonetheless, to embrace the "one at a time" reality to the neglect of the equally important "people of God" dimension of Christ's saving work is surely to miss the Apostle by a great margin.

In this matter Paul is the product of two realities: his own personal history in the Jewish community and his divine appointment to be an apostle to the gentiles (Rom. 1:5; cf. Acts 9:15). Together these led him to presuppose that the goal of God's saving work in Christ is to create an end-time *people* for God's name out of Jews and gentiles together. Paul's passion for such a people finds expression especially in his letters to the believers in Galatia and Rome. It is a primary driving concern in Ephesians as well, where the emphasis is more clearly on the church as a *community* of believers rather than on the salvation of individual believers as such. Indeed, in Ephesians the issue is not on justification by faith at all. The emphasis there is rather singularly on *Jew and gentile* together being re-created into *one people* of God, predicated on the crucifixion and resurrection of Christ and realized by faith and the indwelling of the Spirit.

Similarly, the whole argument of Paul's letter to the believers in Rome climaxes toward the end (15:5–13) with his affirmation as to what God's coming in Christ was all about: "so that with *one mind* and *one voice* you [Jew and gentile together] may glorify the God and Father of our Lord, Jesus Christ" (v. 6). This in turn is followed by a catena of four Old Testament passages (vv. 9–12) whose focus is altogether on the inclusion of the gentiles!

Paul's letter to the believers in Galatia likewise concludes with a repetition of his aphorism, "Neither circumcision nor uncircumcision means anything." It is easy for us twenty centuries later to hear this as ho-hum, but it was anything but for any male Jew in the first century, for whom circumcision would have meant almost everything. But what does count, the Apostle continues, is "a new creation"—which for him meant Jew and gentile together, who are described collectively as "God's Israel." This aphorism made its initial appearance in Paul's first preserved letter to the believers in Corinth,[4] where it is followed by the line: "Keeping God's commands is what counts" (1 Cor. 7:19)! One can only wonder how a

---

4. Paul's preserved correspondence with the Corinthians, which comes to us in the form of 1 and 2 Corinthians, offers evidence of further correspondence between Paul and the Corinthian church that has not been preserved. When I henceforth refer to Paul's first or second letter to the Corinthian church, I refer only to the letters that have been preserved in the New Testament as 1 and 2 Corinthians.

fellow Jew in the community of believers in Corinth might have heard that. It is difficult for us who live in a much different culture, and at a much later time, even to come close to feeling or understanding what a total bombshell such an off-the-cuff statement like that would have been to its original recipients.

At the same time, a believer some twenty centuries later needs also to hear what Paul's own context makes quite clear—that salvation based on *faith* in Christ Jesus assumes also that the believer is expected to *live* in a way that reflects the character of Christ Jesus, just as our Lord himself during his earthly life lived so as to exemplify God's own character. To put it in more contemporary language, the whole purpose of Christ's coming, and of our own salvation, is to re-create a people of God who— redeemed by the Savior Christ and endowed by the Holy Spirit—live out God's original intent. It is to re-create a people who personally and corporately bear the divine likeness in their everyday lives and especially in their relationships with others.

Paul's own calling is expressed in keeping with this concern: "God, who . . . called me by his grace, was pleased to reveal his Son *in me* so that I might preach him among the Gentiles" (Gal. 1:15–16; cf. Rom. 15:15–19). Unfortunately, despite what Paul says so plainly, this sentence has often been misunderstood to mean God's revelation *to* Paul, rather than God's revelation *in* and through Paul's life and calling as an ex- ample of God's grace in this regard. When that key preposition (Gk. *en*) is inaccurately rendered "to" (which occurs in several popular English translations) this rendering quite misses Paul's concern in making this affirmation. His clear point is that he, the Christ hater, was not simply a recipient of that revelation but is himself Exhibit A of God's amazing grace. Thus Paul expresses his self-understanding by echoing language from the prophet Isaiah, who had envisioned the inclusion of the gentiles in the "last days" people of God. This vision of inclusion, which stands at the very beginning of Isaiah (2:2–5), finds expression several times thereafter (11:10; 42:6; 49:6).

Since Isaiah 46:6 and 49:6 appear in Isaiah's so-called Servant Songs, it is not surprising that Paul sees a passage at the beginning of the final Servant Song (54:1) as fulfilled by gentile inclusion (Gal. 4:27), an inclusion found several times elsewhere in the prophetic tradition (Mic.

4:1–2; Zeph. 3:9; Zech. 8:20–22; 14:16–19). This prophetic vision, in turn, takes us back to God's original covenant with Abraham: "I will make you into a great nation . . . and *all peoples on earth* will be blessed through you" (Gen. 12:2–3). Israel's failure in this regard is what is picked up as belonging to the end times by some of the prophets—a tradition to which Paul seems thoroughly indebted.

Luke's version of this calling is given in his account of Paul's final speech in Acts: "I am sending you to the [gentiles] to open their eyes and turn them from darkness to light, and from the power of Satan to God, so that they may receive forgiveness of sins and a place among those who are sanctified by faith in me" (Acts 26:17–18). Although the language is Luke's, the content is fully that of the Apostle and is thus basic to the early believers' understanding of their own role in the great new reality that God was bringing forth. It would take a man like Paul to recognize that by the Spirit God himself had now bridged the gap between Jew and gentile!

Paul's language for the people of God, which now (especially) includes gentiles, is simply an extension of the language of the former covenant. The most common term Paul uses is *hagioi*, "holy ones," which in earlier English versions was rendered "saints." This language was borrowed directly from the book of Daniel (7:18, 22), which itself was an echo of a primary moment in Israel's own history: "Although the whole earth is mine, you will be for me a kingdom of priests and *a holy nation*" (Exod. 19:5–6, *hagios* in the Septuagint).

For those of us reading the English Bible at a later time, however, that rendering has evolved to mean something considerably different from its origins. The word "saint" has become a term used almost exclusively for those who are esteemed as *especially* "holy." As a result we have become accustomed to hearing about "Saint Paul" or "Saint John," but no one under any circumstances would ever refer to the author of this book as "Saint Gordon"! In contrast, for Paul this was standard language for *all* of Christ's people and not just for a special few.

Crucial to this usage for Paul was the promise that "the *holy ones*" would eventually include "all nations and peoples of every language" (Dan. 7:14). Unfortunately, as noted above, this way of referring to the "congregations of the Lord's people" (1 Cor. 14:33), which included *all* believers in a given locale, has evolved in English to refer to an *exclusive* group of believers who are considered to be particularly noteworthy for both their sanctity and their service in behalf of Christ. But the biblical usage must win out. Only as all of those who belong to Christ live in ways in keeping with their Lord himself will the world listen to our gospel.

The same sense of continuity between the Old and New Testaments, between the earlier and present people of God, is found in Paul's usage of the Greek noun *ekklēsia* (lit. "assembly," but most often rendered "church" in English versions). This word also had the advantage of being well known in the Greek world for any gathering of people for a common purpose. In Paul's usage, however, the word was first of all determined by its appearance in the Greek translation of the Old Testament (LXX) as a rendering of the Hebrew word *qahal*. This word was consistently used to refer to the *congregation* of Israel and had to do with the "gathering together" of God's people. It was frequently used, for example, to refer to the assembling of God's people at Mount Sinai.

Thus for Paul there was a happy linguistic coincidence between *qahal* and *ekklēsia* that served as a useful way to tie together the two covenants. This is why the rendering of this word into today's English as "church" is so unfortunate, since for the vast majority of people whose first language is English the word "church" most often connotes a building—a meaning that did not exist at all in Paul's time—rather than a community of believers *gathered together* for worship and fellowship. Indeed, the phrase "going to church" is one of the near travesties of contemporary Protestantism, since we use the same language for "going to" school, "going to" a sporting event, or even "going for" a walk in the park. Rather, Paul's language is meant to encourage us to "assemble" as a church, so as to worship God and Christ as well as to be in fellowship with others.

A similar continuity between Old and New can be found in Paul's use of the terms "election" and "new covenant," both of which occur several times in his various letters. The term "election" appears in both early (1 Thess. 1:4; 2 Thess. 2:12) and later (Col. 3:12; Eph. 1:4, 11) letters and is always a reference to believers, either locally or universally, where the emphasis is simply that God called us to become part of the family of believers. Likewise, the term "new covenant" occurs both early (1 Cor. 11:25; 2 Cor. 3:6–17) and later (Gal. 4:24; Rom. 2:29), in each case echoing a crucial moment in Deuteronomy: "The LORD [= Yahweh] your God will circumcise your hearts and the hearts of your descendants, so that you may love him with all your heart and with all your soul, and live" (30:6).

Equally telling is Paul's use of temple imagery for the people of God in a given location (1 Cor. 3:16–17; 2 Cor. 6:16; Eph. 2:20). This imagery picks up the especially important "presence of God" motif from the Old Testament, which in Galatians 3:28 is explicitly applied to the reality of Jew and gentile together as identifying the one newly formed people of God across three major lines of division: gender (male/female), ethnicity (Jew/gentile), and social status (slave/free). To be sure, Paul did not attack the divisions in social status as such; for him at this moment in history that was simply a given. His singular passion throughout was for a *community* of believers—each one of whom would be some combination of the three identity markers—that their life together would reveal God's character and love for the world.

The Apostle's concern with regard to the people of God is also found in other ways throughout his letters. For example, it is of more than passing interest that most of his letters to churches are addressed to whole congregations, not to a leader or leaders. Indeed, even when leaders are included in the salutation (as in Phil. 1:1), they are so as an addendum: "together with the overseers and deacons." Likewise, when a problem in the church is the direct result of a single individual's wrongdoings, Paul never addresses the wrongdoer directly, and he seldom identifies him or her by name. Rather he calls on the whole church, not just the leaders, to deal with the issue as a community matter. This is especially so in his dealing with the cases of incest and lawsuits in the believing community in Corinth (1 Cor. 5:1–13; 6:1–12). At issue in each of these instances is primarily the *community* as God's newly formed people in Corinth.

Regarding the case of incest, Paul writes, "when you are assembled and I am with you in spirit, and the power of the Lord, Jesus, is present, hand this man over to Satan" (1 Cor. 5:4–5); "get rid of the old yeast so that you may be a new unleavened batch of dough" (v. 7); and finally, "expel the wicked person from among you" (v. 13, using language from Deuteronomy). This sense of corporate social responsibility, which is so often lacking in modern times, lies at the very heart of Paul's understanding of what it means to be the people of God. Especially noteworthy is that this was to be a *community* action, not that of a select group of people in leadership.

The same is true again in the next matter taken up, that of the collective believers' own failure to take on community responsibility when one of their number had brought another brother to court "before the ungodly" (1 Cor. 6:1–6). This kind of action did not take place in a courthouse behind closed doors but would have happened in the Corinthian *agora*, the central "marketplace," and thus in the presence of the whole city, as it were. Paul is incensed and astonished that one of their number felt that to get justice he needed to go to the Roman courts, good as they might have been (and often were in general). "Is it actually possible," he chides, "that there is no one capable of handling such a matter internally" (v. 5) among those who, as followers of the crucified and risen one, should have had a different view of the world and justice?

In this case, Paul finally speaks to the two litigants (in vv. 7–8 and 9–10, respectively), but his primary focus is on what the lawsuit has meant as a failure for the whole community. To be sure, the individual offenders are to be dealt with, but only when the believing community has gathered for worship—that is, in the place where the Spirit of the living God has especially chosen to dwell on earth. In the end, the shame fell on both the one who did the wrong in the first place and the one who, when wronged, chose to redress his grievances outside the community of faith. But for Paul the shame was especially on the community as a whole, among whom the Spirit of the living God had chosen to dwell, but whose actions in so many different ways had become the exact opposite of Christlikeness. Indeed, the community's actions were all too often precisely in keeping with what Paul frequently refers to as "the world" (1 Cor. 1:20–21, 27; 3:19; 6:2; 2 Cor. 10:2–4).

In sum, for Paul salvation in Christ has the creation of *a people for God's name* as its goal, and this concern is especially to be seen in continuity with the people of God as constituted by the former covenant. The eternal God has come to earth as one of us, as the only and finally effective way of re-creating a people for God's name. In Paul's letters this newly formed people are to bear God's character and likeness, both in their individual lives and especially in their common life together in the midst of a fallen and broken world. Our lives as followers of Jesus would be far more faithful and robust if we understood and appreciated the Apostle's passion in these matters and their implications for our own contexts. Unfortunately, rather serious misunderstandings of Paul's concerns have led many to become immune to the radicality of his passions, both for his own churches and for the church today. May we walk more in step with the Spirit, sharing Paul's passions and concerns, to be further conformed to our Lord Jesus Christ as God's people.

A New Creation

Another facet of Paul's soteriology can be seen in his use of "new creation" terminology to speak of the *result* of God's saving event in Christ. Paul expresses this idea not only in terms of "new creation" explicitly but also with his usage of "image of God" and "second Adam" language with regard to Christ. So important is this aspect of Pauline soteriology—especially as it relates to his Christology—that I devote the bulk of chapter 3 to unpacking it. But here I make a few preliminary observations about this language as it pertains to Paul's soteriology in particular.

According to Paul's new creation theology, the death and resurrection of Christ have set in motion a radical, new-order point of view—resurrection life marked by the cross, as Paul explains in the key "new creation" passage in his second letter to the believers in Corinth (2 Cor. 5:14–21). This new viewpoint lies at the heart of everything Paul thinks and does (cf. Phil. 3:4–14), which in turn leads to a series of passages in which Paul picks up "second exodus" imagery from Isaiah 40–66. The eternal God, the prophet proclaims, is about to do a "new thing" (Isa. 43:18–19) and in the end will establish "new heavens and a new earth" (Isa. 65:17; 66:22–23).

In Paul's letters this theme is applied to believers, who through association with Christ's death and resurrection have experienced a form of death and resurrection to newness of life. The theme is expressed in diverse passages, both early and late (Rom. 6:1–14; 7:4–6; Col. 3:1–11; Eph. 4:20–24). Common to these presentations—either explicitly (Rom. 6:1–14) or implicitly (e.g., cf. Col. 2:9–12 with 3:1–11)—is an association with Christian baptism, the key point of entry into the believing community, where "burial" in water symbolizes death to the old and rising to live anew in the world by the power of the Spirit.[5]

In this regard the passage in Colossians is especially noteworthy, since it concludes: "Here there is no Greek and Jew, circumcised and uncircumcised, barbarian, Scythian, slave and free, but Christ is all, and is in all" (Col. 3:11; cf. Gal. 3:28). In the new order already set in motion through Christ's death and resurrection, the value-based distinctions between people—ethnicity, status, and gender—are no longer maintained; all are together sisters and brothers in the same family of God. It is a tragedy that those who consider themselves children of the same heavenly Father, and thus followers of the crucified one, seldom seem genuinely to have caught on to the Apostle's own passions at this point.

In addition to this explicit new-creation language, Paul's use of "image of God" language echoes the primary divine announcement about humankind that appears at the very beginning of the biblical narrative (Gen. 1:26–27). Since God's image-bearers are to be the divinely appointed vice regents in charge of the creation, there is reason to believe that behind this usage is a common feature of suzerainty in the ancient Near East. One way for a suzerain, or sovereign, to remind subject peoples of his sovereignty was by placing images of himself throughout the land as visual reminders of that sovereignty. Thus God expresses his own sovereignty over creation by placing it under those who bear the divine image, man and woman together, created so as to show forth the divine image in their own relationships with one another. What was distorted in the fall was the image of God in humanity; this is precisely where, in Paul's theology, Christ enters history as the one who is bringing about the new creation, restoring the image.

Our Savior is thus the second Adam, the one who, first of all, *in his humanity* is the perfect image-bearer of the eternal God (2 Cor. 4:4; Col. 1:15). At the same time he is the one who *restores that image* in fallen humanity, that is, in those who believe and thus "walk by the Spirit"

---

5. This is also why every form of baptism that has abandoned immersion has given the rite a meaning quite different from that of the Apostle, which tends to focus on becoming members of a given community rather than being identified with Christ through their own form of "death, burial, and resurrection."

(Gal. 5:16). In turn the Spirit empowers those who are born anew to live and behave so as also to reflect the divine image.

In saving a people for God's name, Christ is also described as *ton prōtokon*, "the *firstborn* among many brothers and sisters," who have themselves been predestined to be "conformed into the image of [God's] Son" (Rom. 8:29; cf. Col. 2:10–11). Indeed, as Paul writes elsewhere, it is as though by the Spirit that God's people are looking into a mirror and beholding not their own image but Christ's and are thus being transformed into that same image, from glory to glory, which means either *from present to final glory* or *from one measure of glory to another* (2 Cor. 3:17–18). By the Spirit Christ effects the new creation by restoring humanity back into the divine image.

This divine goal of (re-)creating a people who bear God's image—both individually and collectively—is precisely why Paul instructs believers that, rather than be under the law, they are to "walk by [or in] the Spirit" (Gal. 5:16), and therefore why so much in Paul's extant letters deals with ethical or behavioral matters. As Galatians 5 and Romans 12–14 make abundantly clear, salvation in Christ involves *behavior* on the part of the redeemed ones that reflects God's own character; otherwise for Paul there has been no salvation at all. Indeed, this is the genuinely biblical sense of the old adage, "like Father, like child."

The unfortunate lack of this behavioral dimension of Pauline soteriology—understandably downplayed because of the role of "works" in certain theologies—has been a theological weakness in historical Protestantism. That is, fear of "works" leading to salvation has sometimes resulted in a separation of salvation and ethics. This misses Paul's emphasis on behavior as a matter of being conformed into the image of Christ by the Spirit, having been saved *from* sin *for* new creation life. This is *not* to raise the specter of "works," but it is to note that we are all called to conformity into God's own likeness. Thus Paul's longing for the Galatians is for "Christ [to be] formed in you" (4:19), which in Romans takes the form of an admonition to "clothe yourselves with the Lord, Jesus Christ" (13:14). For Paul, Christlikeness, or restoration into the divine image, is the primary present goal of Christ's "saving work" on our behalf—itself the ultimate restoration of what was lost in Eden.

In the Apostle's theology, therefore, Christ's saving work is both (re-) creating a people for God's name and, at the same time, forming this people to be part of the new creation. Crucial to this understanding of salvation in Christ is that God's newly formed people—both individually and collectively—are to love and serve as God's image-bearers on earth. And this likely is also why Paul's energies seem to be so often (sometimes overwhelmingly so) given to exhorting and encouraging his congregations to live out this calling as God's people wherever they are.

Presupposed in all the Apostle's soteriological talk, as we will see in chapter 2, is both the preexistence and the incarnation of the Son, whose own beginnings were not when he was "born of a woman" (Gal. 4:4). Rather, he was and is eternally the Son, whom the Father *sent* into the world, both to *bear* the divine image and to *restore* that image in God's people as they relate to one another, other people, and the rest of creation. Indeed, it is precisely here that Christology and soteriology intersect in Paul's thinking.

The Place of Christ Devotion in Pauline Theology

This intersection of who Christ is with what Christ did (Christology and soteriology) helps to explain one of the best known, but seldom reflected on, realities in the Pauline corpus: that this rigorous monotheist had become such a devoted follower and worshiper of Christ the Son. This Christ devotion in Paul takes two forms: (1) personal devotion to Christ himself and (2) communal devotion expressed through worship of Christ as Lord. Both of these forms of devotion are full of christological presuppositions.

Christ as the Recipient of Personal Devotion

Having grown up in a devout Diaspora home, Paul would have known by rote the primary commandment for all Israel: "You shall love the LORD [= Yahweh] your God with all your heart." It is therefore interesting that this kind of language occurs only three times in Paul's letters: twice Paul speaks of "those who love" God (1 Cor. 2:9; Rom. 8:28), and in his benediction that concludes the letter to the Ephesians, he extends grace to "all who love our Lord, Jesus Christ" (Eph. 6:24). Despite the paucity of this precise language, the kind of devotion to God the Father that is embraced in this primary commandment is generally given over to Christ the Son in Paul's letters. This finds expression in a variety of ways in his letters, especially whenever he writes longingly of his own and his fellow believers' eschatological future.

It seems that after the Apostle's encounter with the risen Lord, his worldview became thoroughly christocentric, as is demonstrated in the terminology he uses in his letters. In the ten letters in the church corpus, God is mentioned considerably more often than Christ in Romans and slightly more often in 2 Thessalonians and 2 Corinthians; overall Christ is mentioned sixty-three more times than God (599/536), and this appears to be by design. Perhaps most striking with regard to this phenomenon is the way the Apostle can so freely interchange the nouns *Theos* (God) and *Christos* (Christ) in a variety of ways when speaking about divine activities.

This Christ devotion is a rather striking feature in light of Paul's otherwise rather consistent grammar of salvation expressed most notably in one of his early letters (1 Cor. 8:6). Here Paul had reworked the Jewish Shema to include Christ, so that the "one God" (the source and goal of all things) is the Father, and the "one LORD" (Yahweh, who is the divine agent of all things) is Christ Jesus. And, significantly, in Paul's worldview both the source and goal of all things and the divine agent of all things are to be worshiped as one.

In Paul's radically changed worldview following his encounter with the risen Lord, therefore, almost everything is done in relation to Christ. The believing communities exist "in Christ," and everything believers are and do is "for Christ," "by Christ," "through Christ," and "for the sake of Christ." And these more generalized expressions of life totally devoted to Christ also at times find more specific expression. Take, for example, the Apostle's argument with the Corinthians as to the advantages of the single life. Such people are "concerned about the Lord's affairs—how they can please the Lord," and their "aim is to be devoted to the Lord in both body and spirit" (1 Cor. 7:32, 34). Indeed, being single allows one the best of all options: "to live in a right way in undivided devotion to the Lord" (v. 35). It is not difficult to hear Paul speaking personally here, even though he presents this as a viable option for the unmarried in Corinth. In our fascination with the matter of marriage and singleness, the christological focus of his argument should not be passed over, for at the center of all such instruction and admonition is "the Lord" (= Christ Jesus).

Similarly, where the Old Testament precedent had put emphasis on Israel "knowing God," this kind of language appears in Paul only with relation to Christ. This is especially so in Philippians, where the kind of longing that Paul has for these friends is placed "in the bowels [= affection] of Christ Jesus" (1:8). When he goes on to tell his own story as a model of a cruciform life (3:4–14), he echoes an especially crucial Yahweh moment from the prophet Jeremiah: "Let the one who boasts, boast about this: 'that they have understanding to know me, that I am the Lord'" (Jer. 9:24). Paul claims that the Lord in whom he boasts is Christ Jesus. Indeed, he continues: "I consider everything a loss because of the surpassing worth of *knowing Christ Jesus my Lord*" (Phil. 3:8). Here the identification of "the Lord," which in Jeremiah refers to Yahweh, is transferred completely to Christ. The christological significance of this can scarcely be gainsaid, since these words are written by one whose religious heritage includes the Psalter, where this kind of devotion is offered exclusively to Yahweh. In Paul such devotion to God is expressed *primarily* for Christ, in the sense that it appears this way in his letters more frequently than otherwise. As such passages indicate, Paul acts and talks like a trinitarian well before that language had become a part of the believers' vocabulary.

Paul's longing for the arrival of God's eschatological future is best understood in light of such Christ devotion. In Paul's letters this longing finds expression exclusively in terms of being "with Christ" and never expressly as being "with God," although one may well assume that such an understanding is inherent in his longing for Christ. This phenomenon begins in his earliest letters. He writes to the Thessalonians: "we wait for his Son from heaven" so that "we may live with him," whom "we will be with forever" (1 Thess. 1:10; 5:10; 4:17). Likewise, in his next letter to them he writes of "our being gathered to him" (2 Thess. 2:1). In his second letter to the Corinthians, he writes that the "eternal glory that outweighs" present suffering is expressed in terms of "being away from the body [in its present suffering] and at home with the Lord [with a body 'overclothed' for eternity]" (2 Cor. 4:17; 5:8). And in one of his latest letters, Paul writes of his desire to "depart and be with Christ" (Phil. 1:23). Thus Paul's Christ devotion can be seen from beginning to end.

Again, Paul writes nothing similar about being with God the Father. It is thus hardly surprising that one of the later expressions of the standard benediction with which Paul's letters conclude takes the form, "Grace to all who love our Lord, Jesus Christ" (Eph. 5:24). While such an expression seems natural enough to those of us who have been raised on the Christian Scriptures and frequently worship in Christian churches, it is striking when read in its original context. Here is a thoroughgoing monotheist, raised in a context that was absolutely God-centered, who now turns the larger part of his own personal devotion to the Lord, *Jesus Christ*.

That Paul seems to simply assume such a Christology in his personal devotion is significant—as significant, if not more so, than his explicitly christological affirmations. It would be one thing if Paul were trying to establish or argue for such a point of view, but instead it is *from* this reality—assumed by both Paul and his converts—that he argues for every kind of virtue in a life lived in obedience to Christ. Christology can scarcely get higher than this!

Christ as the Object of Community Worship

Christ devotion as direct worship takes several forms in Paul's letters, probably as the direct result of the early believers' devotion to the risen Christ, which itself likely began around the meal eaten in honor of Christ. Indeed, on one occasion the Apostle refers to this meal as the "Lord's table" (1 Cor. 10:21). We now look in more detail at three expressions of such devotion that have christological implications: celebrating at the Lord's table, singing hymns to and about Christ, and addressing prayers to Christ.

The Lord's Table

The central role that the Lord's table assumed in the early church is a most remarkable christological innovation. Interestingly, it is something we know about in the Pauline churches only because of a Corinthian abuse. In the entire corpus of Paul's preserved letters, it is mentioned or alluded to only in Paul's first letter to Corinth—and there no less than four times (1 Cor. 10:3–4, 16–17; 11:17–34; 5:8).

In 1 Corinthians 10:3–4, Paul alludes to the Christian table by way of an analogy with the food and drink divinely supplied to Israel in the desert. This analogy is almost certainly expressed in anticipation of what Paul will say a bit later (10:16–17), where he speaks of the Lord's table as the exclusively Christian meal, which thereby forbids attendance at the meals in the idol/demon temples. Israel, Paul points out, had its own form of divinely supplied food and drink, yet that did not "secure" them with God, and because of their idolatries, the vast majority of them were "scattered in the wilderness" (10:3–10). In the process of this argument Paul eventually interprets the bread as having to do with *the church*— "we who are many"—as Christ's body (v. 17). In so doing he anticipates the issue of unity and diversity, which he will address later in the letter (chaps. 12–14). All of this puts the focus of the Christian meal squarely on the Lord, Jesus Christ.

But most subsequent interest in what Paul says about what came to be called the Eucharist (Greek for "thanksgiving") has focused on the issue and remedy that he speaks to in 1 Corinthians 11:17–34, where apparently the more well-to-do were abusing those who were poorer by turning the table celebration into their own private meal that excluded "those who have nothing." To correct this abuse Paul reminds them of the words of institution, which are nearly identical to those found in Luke's Gospel. What is especially significant about this passage for our present christological interests is that there can be little question that the meal described is *the Christian version of a meal in honor of a deity*. We can observe this in four ways from this passage.

First, Paul's language for the meal in this instance is "the *Lord's* Supper" (1 Cor. 11:20), language that occurs only here in the New Testament. This is likely a Pauline construct deliberately chosen in contrast to what Paul goes on to call "your own private suppers." Almost certainly this refers to those who were better off financially and socially than many of the other believers. Of special interest for our purposes is the word Paul uses to refer to Christ, the adjective *kyriakon*, which can mean either "pertaining to" ("in honor of") or "belonging to" the Lord, meaning that it is his own specifically instituted meal. But in either case Paul's own language puts the emphasis on the fact that this meal uniquely has to do with "the Lord," in whose name and honor it is eaten. Thus, as with the Passover in Israel, which this meal is modeled after, this is the only singularly Christian meal, and the focus and honor now belongs to the "Lord" (Jesus) rather than to God the Father.

Second, this meal was instituted by Christ in the context of a Passover meal, as Paul expresses in two ways. First, in 1 Corinthians 5:7–8 in his discussion of the case of incest in the church, he asserts, "Christ, our Passover lamb, has been sacrificed. Therefore let us keep the Festival, not with the old bread leavened with malice and wickedness" (and thus without the incestuous man present). Such language can only be an allusion to the Lord's table and thus to Paul's understanding of the connection between what Christ did and the Christian celebration of their own feast. Also, in 1 Corinthians 11:23, Paul uses the introductory phrase, "on the night he was betrayed," an allusion to Jesus's institution of this meal in the context of the Passover.

Paul's concern seems clear: that in the Christian community the Passover meal formerly eaten annually in honor of Yahweh, and in remembrance of the deliverance of his people from Egypt, is now eaten regularly (probably weekly) and exclusively in honor of Christ as the Christian *deity*, and thus in remembrance of his delivering his people from bondage to Satan. Again, it is nearly impossible to imagine a Christology higher than this!

Third, in the earlier reference to the meal (1 Cor. 10), Paul deliberately set the meal in honor of the Lord as the Christian alternative to the pagan temple meals, which some of the Corinthians were insisting on attending since, according to the Shema, there is only one true God. Apparently in their view, the pagan meals, even though in honor of a deity, were not *in reality* in honor of a deity since the "god" did not actually exist. To be sure, Paul grants them that there is only one true God; nonetheless, he identifies the "deities" as demons (v. 20), thus acknowledging their reality.

In so doing Paul is clearly setting out the Lord's table as the Christian alternative to these pagan meals; at the same time he also assumes that Christ is the Christian *deity* who is honored at his meal. It would be simply unthinkable to have such a meal in honor of a mere human who sacrificed himself on behalf of others and who was therefore highly honored by God through resurrection. Indeed, these offhand comments that reveal Paul's presuppositions are probably the most telling evidence not only that Paul holds a high Christology himself but also that he *assumes* it is shared by the believing communities that he has founded—and this within two decades of the cross and resurrection!

Fourth, the remainder of Paul's corrective puts the Corinthian abuse in the strongest possible christological framework. Abuse of the Lord's body (= the church) at the Lord's table has resulted in divine punishment. Significantly, these sentences also make plain that the present judgments are to be understood as coming from the *deity* who is being dishonored, namely, "the Lord" (1 Cor. 11:32), Jesus Christ. The net result is that a meal in honor of the Lord calls for the Lord's judgment on those who would abuse his people—who corporately bear the divine *eikōn*, or image—at his table.

From Paul's Jewish worldview, the prerogative to judge belongs to God alone. Again, all of this is in place as the assumed common ground between the Apostle and these believers, which so incontrovertibly reveals Paul's thoroughgoing theological understanding of Christ. Thus everything about Paul's discussion of the Lord's table either assumes or asserts the highest kind of Christology in relationship to Christ as *divine* Savior.

Singing Hymns to Christ

As in his discussion of the Lord's Supper, Paul almost incidentally reminds the believers in Colossae that singing hymns in Christian worship has the message *about* Christ as its primary focus: "Let the message of Christ dwell among you richly as you *teach* and *admonish* one another with all wisdom through psalms, hymns, and songs from the Spirit, singing to God with gratitude in your hearts" (Col. 3:16). Thus singing lay at the heart of Christian worship from the very beginning, and such singing is full of assumed Christology. Hymns like those preserved in the Psalter that were both "to" and "about" Yahweh are now sung (apparently exclusively) to and about Christ Jesus.

In Colossians 3:16 the primary concern of the exhortation is with the "message of Christ," that is, the message of the gospel with its central focus on Christ. As with the Jewish Psalter, so with the believers in Colossae: what is most truly believed about Christ is regularly reaffirmed through singing hymns to him or in his name. Thus the concern in these affirmations is not on Christ speaking *to* them as they gather—although that too could happen through prophetic utterance—or with his teachings; rather, as Paul declares at the outset of the letter, his primary concern is the message of the gospel with its total focus on Christ. Indeed, this is what the letter is all about: Christ as the creator, the redeemer, and the embodiment of God. Paul now urges that this "message of Christ"— which in part he had articulated in 1:15–23—"dwell among you" in an abundant way. In so doing, part of the believers' activity will be directed toward one another ("teach[ing] and admonish[ing] one another"), and part toward God ("singing to God with gratitude in your hearts"). Thus the gospel is to be present among them "richly." The structure of 3:16 as a whole indicates that songs of all kinds—with Christ now as their focus and content—are to play a significant role in that richness.

Significantly, it is likely, as most scholars now assume, that Paul's earlier words about Christ in this letter (1:15–18), which focus on our Savior and his work, reflect an early Christian hymn. If so, that would explain why Paul thinks of these various kinds of hymns and Spirit songs as a way the believers can "teach and admonish one another." Such songs are by their very nature creedal, full of theological grist, and thus give evidence of what the early Christians most truly believed about both God and Christ.

In the twin passage in Ephesians 5:18–19, the exhortation turns to singing hymns *to* Christ. The background to the two-dimensional worship expressed here and assumed in the Colossians passage—hymns that are at once directed toward the deity and didactic for the participants—is found in the Jewish Psalter. There we find dozens of examples of hymns addressed to God in the second person, which also have sections in the third person extolling the greatness or faithfulness of God for the sake of those singing to God. The use of hymns in the New Testament indicates how much they function for the early church in this two-dimensional way. In the Pauline churches in particular, Christ often assumes the dual role of being sung to and sung about. Again, the seemingly incidental or unselfconscious way that Paul transfers the Psalter's pattern to Christian hymns further supports the view that devotion previously given exclusively to Yahweh has for the early Christians transferred to Christ as "Lord"—to the one who came to earth to both redeem and re-create us into the divine image.

In sum, as with the Lord's table, worship in the form of singing focuses on Christ as the centerpiece. The singing contains the message *about* Christ and is at times sung *to* Christ as well. Such worship as this includes Christ as divine, while always maintaining unwavering monotheism. Once again, such presuppositional high Christology is often more telling than explicit christological statements.

Prayer

The third form of the worship of Christ the Savior as Lord comes in the form of prayer directed toward Christ in precisely the same ways that prayer is also directed toward God the Father. This pattern appears in the first two letters in the Pauline corpus, 1 and 2 Thessalonians, and continues right to the end (for those who consider 1 and 2 Timothy as the end of the Pauline corpus).

The evidence for this is writ large throughout the thirteen Pauline letters and covers most kinds of prayer, although some scholars have played down the role of Christ in prayer, which can only be done by sidestepping the considerable evidence to the contrary. Had Christ *not* been included as the object in these passages, then all would see them as true prayers addressed to God. But because Christ is the object in these passages, some scholars have argued that we should not read them as prayers. But in reality these patterns follow the same pattern we have seen above: Paul prays *to* Christ in precisely the same way he does to God the Father.

Thus, in Paul's benedictory prayers, which occur most frequently in the two letters to the Thessalonians, Paul directs his prayer to both God and Christ. In 1 Thessalonians he directs his prayer first to *God and Christ together* (with a singular verb), that *they* would "clear the way for us to come to you" (1 Thess. 3:11). This is immediately followed by prayer to Christ alone (vv. 12–13), that he would cause the Thessalonian Christians to increase and abound in love, both for one another and for all, and would also "strengthen your hearts" toward blameless and holy living. In 2 Thessalonians Paul does the same thing in reverse, directing the prayer to *Christ and God together* (again with a verb in the singular) but following with prayer directed toward God alone (2 Thess. 2:16–17). Then in two concluding prayers of this kind (2 Thess. 3:5, 16), *only* Christ is addressed. Once again, Paul is not here *asserting* something about Christ as to his deity; rather, he is clearly and simply *assuming* it—and he is doing this in such a way that he does not expect it to catch his readers' special attention in some way. Again, the offhanded way this happens—and in this case happens so early—is striking evidence of Paul's high Christology.

The same phenomenon can be seen in Paul's letters to the Corinthians, both in more direct prayer and in his reports of his prayers. Thus in more direct prayer Paul concludes his first letter to the believers in Corinth with the (apparently) universal language of early Christian prayer, *Marana tha*, "Come, Lord" (1 Cor. 16:22). In his next letter to them he reports that he specifically petitioned Christ as Lord to remove the "thorn in [his] flesh" (2 Cor. 12:7) and that Christ answered: "My grace is sufficient for you" (2 Cor. 12:9). Here again Paul is *not* trying to make a point about Christ's deity. He is simply doing what has become natural for him: addressing prayer to Christ as often as to God the Father—and sometimes to both together. Deity is simply presupposed in such moments. And as Larry Hurtado has pointed out, such Christ devotion is in many ways more telling theologically than actual theological statements themselves.[6] Devotion to Christ was simply taken for granted well before the earliest known statements about Christ emerged in the early Christian community. Both the acclamation by the Spirit that "Jesus is Lord" (1 Cor. 12:3) and the *Marana tha* prayer (1 Cor. 16:22) precede any known attempts to express theologically the implications of such Christ devotion, and the latter surely arise out of the former.

6. See Larry W. Hurtado, *Lord Jesus Christ: Devotion to Jesus in Earliest Christianity* (Grand Rapids: Eerdmans, 2003); Hurtado, *How on Earth Did Jesus Become God? Historical Questions about Earliest Devotion to Jesus* (Grand Rapids: Eerdmans, 2005).

Conclusion

For Paul, Christ the Savior is not just the *mediator of salvation*. Christ the Savior also emerges as the ongoing *object of devotion* and *worship* in the Pauline corpus—both for Paul and for his churches. Moreover, the worship is not only because of *what Christ did* for us but also, and especially, because of *who he is* as divine Savior.

Paul's letters make clear that Christ's significance as divine Savior did not *begin* with his earthly life as Jesus of Nazareth. Rather, that earthly life was an expression of an incarnation of the preexistent Son of God. Paul understands the exalted Son of God to be Lord of all, but he also presupposes that the Savior *came to earth* to redeem—language that assumes not simply birth as such but also *incarnation*, the birth of one who was fully divine. In order to understand the christological significance of Christ as divine Savior, then, we must come to terms with Paul's understanding of the divine Savior as both preexistent and incarnate—and in that incarnation truly human in every aspect of our humanity but without sin. We turn to these matters in chapter 2.

2

The Preexistent and Incarnate Savior

On several occasions in his letters, Paul either asserts or assumes the preexistence of Christ as the eternal Son of God. For Paul these affirmations are not offered as abstract speculations about Christ's nature but, in most instances, are expressed in sentences that speak of Christ's *saving* activity. In so doing, they combine soteriology and Christology, pointing to the reality that Christ is not simply our Savior but also the *divine* Savior—crucified, buried, and raised from the dead for the sake of the entire human race! Below we examine these passages in detail, but first we must note the theological significance of the *nature* of these passages.

The Nature of Paul's Incarnational Christology

Perhaps the most significant feature of Paul's incarnational theology is the absence of a single instance in Paul's letters in which he tries to *demonstrate* or *argue for* preexistence and incarnation. Indeed, quite the opposite is true: in every case Paul argues for something else predicated on the affirmations of preexistence and incarnation that he and his readers already hold in common. The cumulative effect of this pattern across Paul's corpus carries considerable christological weight. Were

Paul arguing *for* an incarnation, then one could pursue him with regard to both what he is arguing and how he is arguing it, as to whether his arguments work or are weighty. But when he simply presupposes these realities and thus repeatedly argues *from* them, the issue becomes not whether Paul and his churches believed in Christ as the divine, pre-existent Savior but rather what the nature and content of the belief they all held in common was.

To be sure, because of the way these various affirmations come to us, it is conceivable to argue (and indeed has been argued) for a nonincarnational reading of any given passage. But such an approach works only for those who set out beforehand to demonstrate such a reading. The conclusions in every case are the result of looking at any one passage in isolation from the others and then arguing that what Paul says in that passage does not necessarily assert or assume preexistence. This is the old divide-and-conquer approach. Instead of reading each of Paul's affirmations in its original context, as well as in light of the others, one sets out with a prior agenda to demonstrate that no single one of the texts in which the church—and scholars—have historically found preexistence necessarily *requires* such a view. Then, by showing how a given passage might possibly be understood in another way, one argues that it therefore probably does not affirm or even imply preexistence.

But any interpretation is suspect if its primary goal is to get around what Paul appears plainly to have presupposed, especially when such an interpretation involves an accumulation of otherwise disparate sentences in Paul's several letters written over a fifteen-year span. It is one thing to look at any one of his sentences in its own context in isolation from the others and then to argue that this particular case does not necessarily *require* preexistence. Such an interpretation would still require a considerable stretch regarding what the Apostle intended for his own readers, but it might have a certain level of plausibility. But it is another thing to argue against both the cumulative effect of the several passages together and the presuppositional nature of each within the context of the affirmation, for along with the explicit affirmations in each instance, the presuppositional reality behind them forcefully calls into question any interpretation that denies preexistence. To feel the full weight of the cumulative effect of these passages, we examine them below under three headings: Christ as the agent of creation and redemption; Christ as impoverished redeemer; and Christ the Son as the sent one.

Christ as the Agent of Creation and Redemption

Two passages describe Christ as the agent of creation and redemption: 1 Corinthians 8:6 and Colossians 1:15–20. While each passage has its own distinct context—the first passage written quite early and the second written a few years later—what they have in common is language of creation and redemption taking place *through* Christ. And in each case these observations are offered for pragmatic reasons.

1 CORINTHIANS 8:6

Yet for us there is but one God, the Father, from whom all things came and for whom we live; and there is but one Lord, Jesus Christ, through whom all things came and through whom we live.

In one of the more striking affirmations in the entire collection of Pauline letters, Paul reshapes the primary affirmation of his own Jewish heritage, the Shema (Deut. 6:4), to embrace both Father and Son. While at the same time emphasizing his inherited monotheism, that there is only "one God," Paul asserts that the "one Lord" (= Yahweh) of the Shema is now to be identified as the Lord, Jesus Christ. And he does this in a context where he is both agreeing with and deliberately enlarging the perspective of the believers in Corinth.

While still embracing a version of rigorous monotheism, some of the Corinthian believers were arguing for the right to attend the meals with friends in the precincts of the pagan temples, where "deities" of various kinds were honored. Apparently their right to do so was being justified on the basis of that monotheism (since the "god" did not actually exist, how could one forbid it?). Paul is in full agreement with them on the first matter (rigid monotheism), but he will have none of their further argument based on that affirmation. As was noted in our discussion of the Lord's table in chapter 1, Paul eventually rejects their spurious reasoning on theological grounds, asserting that the "gods" are the habitations of demons (1 Cor. 10:14–22).

But at this earlier moment in the letter, Paul's use and elaboration of the Shema is for the sake of those in the believing community, the "weak brother or sister," for whom the divine Son had died and been raised (1 Cor. 8:11). Because of prior associations with these meals in the context of a nonexistent "god," such believers could not attend these temple meals without being "destroyed." For them it was a matter of considerable, and understandable, dissonance between the head and the heart, between what could be argued intellectually but not be pushed aside experientially. Paul's response in this case is a most remarkable moment, and it provides a piece of the raw data that made the church's eventual articulation of trinitarian theology necessary.

Paul's assertion that the same Christ who redeems also had the prior role of preexistent creator serves as a backdrop for Paul's argument two chapters later that the Israelites tested "Christ" in the desert (1 Cor. 10:9). The Corinthian believers, he insists, are in similar danger as were the Israelites, many of whom died in the desert as a result of their immorality. The preexistent Christ, Paul argues, was with Israel as the "rock that accompanied them" and was responsible for many of them being killed by snakes (10:4, 9). The explicit point of Paul's argument is that, if Christ's presence did not guarantee Israel's entrance into the promised land, the Corinthian believers need to take heed regarding the possible consequences of their own flirtation with idolatry.

At the same time—in a more profoundly theological way, by including the preexistent Son as the agent of creation—Paul has included Christ in the divine identity at its most fundamental point: as the one God the Jews regularly identified vis-à-vis all other "gods" as the creator and ruler of all things. It is one thing for Christ to be the means of redemption, but for Paul to likewise declare Christ to be the divine agent of creation is clearly to include Christ within Paul's new understanding of the "one God" of the Shema. Indeed, Paul's frequent appellation of God as Father has its origins not with God as *our* Father but with Yahweh's newly understood identity as "the God and Father of our Lord, Jesus Christ" (2 Cor. 11:31; Eph. 1:3). Hence, Paul's identification of the "one God" in this passage with "*the* Father" presupposes Christ as "*the* Son."

That Paul so easily, and in such a matter-of-fact way, enlarges the Shema to embrace Christ would seem to indicate that his view of God's oneness as including both Father and Son did not begin with this ad hoc statement. Everything about his presuppositional way of communicating this indicates quite the opposite: that this is a theological standpoint already held in common by both Paul and his readers, *from* which Paul goes on to address various practical matters. This affirmation therefore functions as the theological basis for the behavioral concerns he is now addressing. The Apostle here simply assumes common ground with his readers on this point, which then serves as the basis from which to argue with them about those matters that they do not share in common. Moreover, it is significant that, on one level, this striking christological assertion is unnecessary for Paul to make his argument with the Corinthians, precisely because nothing *christological* is at stake here. Indeed, in a later letter, in a doxology directed toward God alone (Rom. 11:36), the phrase "from him and through him and for him are all things" appears without this christological modification.

Yet the perfect poetic parallel in 1 Corinthians 8:6 suggests that this is not the first time Paul has found a way to hold together two significant realities: his fundamental and unwavering monotheism and his inclusion of Christ in the divine identity. This is the earliest, and one of the most intriguing, instances of Paul's clear assertion of Christ as the *preexistent* Son of God—and its earliest occurrence in the New Testament. But the overt reason for this assertion is not to establish its reality but to address concern for the "weak" believers in Corinth, that they not be abused by the "knowledge" of some others within the community of faith (8:11). Again, it is not something Paul is arguing *for* but something he is arguing *from*, as assumed common ground between him and his audience, which suggests that it is a basic theological affirmation held in common by the entire early church. Whereas myths and legends are the product of generations of folklore, we can be fairly confident that the affirmation of Christ's preexistence was fully in place within the first two decades of the Christian faith.

To be sure, some have tried to get around this plain assertion of Christ's preexistence by suggesting that the whole passage is merely soteriological and not dealing with ontology (the question of being) or by identifying Christ with personified Wisdom and thus asserting that only Wisdom preexisted. But there is not a hint of personified Wisdom in this passage, and to insert that notion into the picture here borders on absurdity. After all, Paul's assertion at the very outset of his letter—that a *crucified Messiah* is God's power *and wisdom* vis-à-vis the Corinthians' own fascination with Greek wisdom—undercuts the idea that Paul identifies Christ with so-called Lady Wisdom, which would have been beyond the original readers' capacity to understand. Moreover, the argument that these texts are about Lady Wisdom instead of the preexistence of Christ faces enormous exegetical difficulties, since Wisdom is never posited in the Wisdom literature as the actual agent of creation. Indeed, when Wisdom literature personifies Wisdom in such passages, she is envisioned as only *present* at creation, as evidenced by creation's wise design (e.g., Prov. 8:22–31). In contrast, Christ is here identified not just as present at creation but as the very agent of creation.

COLOSSIANS 1:15–20

For the Son is the image of the invisible God, the firstborn over all creation. For in him all things were created: things in heaven and on earth, visible and invisible, whether thrones or powers or rulers or authorities; *all things have been created through him and for him.* He is before all things, and in him all things hold together.

And he is the head of his body, the church; he is the beginning and the firstborn from among the dead, so that in everything he might have the supremacy. For God was pleased to have all his fullness dwell in him, and *through him to reconcile to himself all things,* whether things on earth or things in heaven, by making peace through his blood, shed on the cross.

In a poem of two stanzas toward the beginning of his letter to the believers in Colossae, which looks very much like an elaboration of the two lines of affirmation in his earlier letter to the Corinthians, Paul once again asserts that the Son of God is the divine agent of both creation and redemption. However, in this case the two lines are now elaborated in such a way as to place Christ at the beginning point of both the old and the new creations.

In this case, Christ is explicitly identified as the beloved Son of the Father (Col. 1:13), who both bears the "image" of the unseen God (v. 15) and is the efficient cause and goal of the whole created order (v. 16). At the same time, as Son he assumes the role of God's own "firstborn"—with regard to both creation (v. 15) and resurrection (v. 18). This Son, who is thus the "beginning" of the new creation (v. 18) as he was agent of the first, has reconciled all things *to himself* "by making peace through his blood, shed on the cross" (v. 20). The net result is that even divine reconciliation was not simply achieved *by* him but was also reconciliation *to* him.

So intent is Paul in placing Christ as supreme—and thus above the "powers" (Col. 1:16)—that he elaborates the Son's role in creation in two ways: first, by using two of the three prepositions that in an earlier letter he had used of God the Father (*through, for;* Rom. 11:36), and second, by twice using the all-embracing *in him*, regarding the Son's role both in creating and sustaining the world. Christ the Son is thus simultaneously both the *creator* of all things and the *sphere* in which all created things have their existence.

To state Paul's affirmations emphatically, it is the Son who is the image of the unseen God; it is the Son who has the rights of the firstborn; it is the Son through whom and in whom all things came to be; and it is the Son who, by virtue of his resurrection, stands as the beginning of the new creation, effected through his reconciling death. Paul's affirmations are so plain and emphatic here that the only way some have tried to get around them has been to deny Pauline authorship of the letter. But that is the ultimate counsel of despair: to make an underling genius "out-Paul" Paul!

Paul's christocentric emphasis continues into the stanza regarding redemption, where there is an equal emphasis on incarnation. Using the enlarged expression "all his fullness," meaning all the divine fullness that is inherent to the one and only God, Paul asserts that this "fullness" likewise dwelt in our Savior so that, as the incarnate one, Christ might reconcile *all things to himself*—and thus, by implication, to God.

Since Paul did not found the church in Colossae, he spells out in some detail the more condensed assertion in his earlier letter to the believers in Corinth discussed above (1 Cor. 8:6). This creates the interesting phenomenon that, while the passage as a whole has an assumptive ring to it, it provides the closest thing one finds in the Apostle's letters to a deliberate presentation of Paul's assumed Christology. Thus both its poetic nature and the insertion of the phrases about the powers (Col.

1:16) indicate that he is still presenting Christ in a way that assumes he and the recipients are on common ground.

For in Christ all the fullness of the Deity lives in bodily form.

When Paul turns his attention to the Colossian situation itself, he begins with a series of imperatives. First, and positively, the believers are to "live [their] lives in" Christ, whom they have "received" (Col. 2:6). Second, and negatively, they are to beware the "hollow and deceptive philosophy" that is currently threatening them, "which depends on human tradition and the elemental spiritual forces of this world rather than on Christ" (2:8).

When he then goes on to identify what it means to be dependent on Christ, Paul returns to what he posited earlier (Col. 1:19), but now with special emphasis on the incarnation. "In Christ," he asserts again, "all the fullness of the Deity lives in *bodily* form" (2:9). Such a condensed phrase seems clearly to assume the emphasis on preexistence expressed in the earlier poetry (1:15–20), which he has now elaborated by emphasizing the genuinely incarnational dimension of Christ as the divine presence while on earth.

How this relates to the Colossian error itself has been a matter of some debate and speculation. But whatever their error may have been, Paul's addition of the word "bodily" denies any spiritual understanding of Christ that does not embrace an actual incarnation. Although preexistence is not made explicit here, given the preceding passage in the letter, which places the Son as the agent of both creation and redemption, it seems that preexistence is absolutely presuppositional to what Paul is urging throughout the letter.

Christ as Impoverished Redeemer

The second way Paul assumes Christ's preexistence as a part of his argument comes in two passages where Paul speaks of the incarnation with extraordinarily strong metaphorical language: 2 Corinthians 8:9 and Philippians 2:6–8. In both instances the emphasis of the metaphor is on the impoverishment that Christ experienced by becoming human. In each passage Paul presents Christ as an exemplary paradigm for the conduct being urged on his readers. Here especially the metaphors are too strong, and the language too plain, to allow any interpretation that discounts preexistence and incarnation.

2 CORINTHIANS 8:9

For you know the grace of our Lord, Jesus Christ, that though he was rich, yet for your sakes he became poor, so that you through his poverty might become rich.

Paul reminds the Corinthians of the character of Christ as part of his final appeal to them to follow through on their commitment to help provide for the poor in Jerusalem. In trying to avoid any semblance of command or coercion, he asserts that his concern is that their actions will demonstrate the sincerity of their love. Paul's final coup is to speak in metaphor of Christ's incarnation and redemption for their sakes: "For you know the grace of our Lord, Jesus Christ, that though he was rich, yet *for your sakes he became poor*, so that you *through his poverty* might become rich." Here the clause "for your sakes he became poor" is a metaphor for the incarnation, and the clause "so that you through his poverty might become rich" is likewise a metaphor for the crucifixion and its benefits for the Corinthians.

In keeping with the money issue at hand—and as Christ's own expression of grace—Paul appeals directly to the enormous generosity of the Savior's incarnation (which in turn leads to his crucifixion). The appearance on earth of the One who was preexistent as God can be expressed only in terms of his becoming poor, an impoverishment that meant untold riches for others (including the Corinthians). But, Paul argues, his aim is not their own impoverishment; rather, it is simply that, given the enormity of Christ's generosity, they should gladly follow through on their commitment to the poor, which will not impoverish them in any way.

Again, this metaphor works only because Paul and the Corinthians share the same presuppositional understanding of Christ as the preexistent One who became incarnate. This very tight metaphorical sentence (which would break down if elaborated) was written to the same community to whom Paul had formerly written that most remarkable restatement of the Jewish Shema to include both Father and Son (1 Cor. 8:6).

PHILIPPIANS 2:6–8

Who, being in very nature God, did not consider equality with God something to be used to his own advantage; rather, he made himself nothing by taking the very nature of a servant, being made in human likeness. And being found in appearance as a man, he humbled himself by becoming obedient to death—even death on a cross!

Paul retells the Christ story in Philippians 2:6–11 primarily to reinforce by way of divine example some attitudinal concerns Paul has regarding internal relationships in the believing community in Philippi. "Do nothing," he has urged, "out of selfish ambition or vain conceit" (v. 3). Rather, they are to have the opposite mind-set, that which is exemplified by Christ through both his incarnation (vv. 6–7) and his crucifixion (v. 8).

With the imitation of Christ as Paul's goal, he tells Christ's story in particularly powerful and telling language. Beginning with the Savior's prior existence "in very nature God" (Phil. 2:6), Paul urges that this equality with God was not in Christ's case exemplified by his selfishly grasping or holding on to what was rightly his. To the contrary, and now with an especially strong metaphor, Paul asserts that Christ chose (literally) "to pour himself out" with regard to his equality with God by assuming the "form of a slave" with regard to his incarnation (v. 7). To clarify what this means, Paul then abandons the metaphors regarding Christ's divine preexistence and says it plainly: "being made in human likeness," or more literally, "coming to be in human likeness" (v. 7).

Paul then emphasizes the reality of Christ's incarnation by starting the next sentence with an echo of the preceding one, which repeats the emphasis on the genuineness of Christ's humanity. It was as the one who was "found in appearance as a man" that Christ humbled himself to the Father in an obedience that led to death on a cross (Phil. 2:8).

These verses have turned out to be some of the more difficult in the New Testament to render into adequate English. Paul's intention seems clear enough—to use Christ's incarnation and crucifixion as an exemplary paradigm for the believers in Philippi to emulate—but it is not the details they are to emulate but the attitudinal basis for Christ's action on their behalf. Just as Christ emptied himself for the sake of those he loves, so too Paul writes the Philippians: "In humility value others above yourselves, not looking to your own interests, but each of you to the interests of the others" (Phil. 2:3–4). Any reading of this passage that does not take seriously its implied and expressed emphasis on Christ's incarnation is a reading of the text apart from the context in which Paul has told the story. Moreover, both the grammar and content of the passage disallow any other reading.

Some scholars have argued that Paul here intends to echo the story of Adam, but such a view makes no sense in light of what the Apostle affirms. It misses the context of the argument and misses, crucially, that Adam was neither said to be in the form of God nor said to be equal with God. By yielding to sin, Adam was not said to have poured himself out into the slavery of his fallenness and thus to have found himself to be a fallen human. If an echo of Eden from Genesis 2–3 is present at all in this passage, it is only conceptual: Christ, who had divine status, chose to become a human, while Eve and Adam, having been created in the divine image, sought for a divine privilege, which became their undoing. But to push the analogy further than that requires considerable ingenuity and the ability to read back into the Genesis narrative what is neither explicit nor implicit in the narrative itself. One who already is only and merely human (Adam) does not *become* human as our Savior did in his incarnation.

As with the previous passages we have considered, so too here Paul can make use of Christ as the exemplary paradigm precisely because this is a belief he shares with the letter's recipients. When one considers that the church in Philippi was founded in the late 40s CE (that is, less than two decades after the cross and resurrection), one must further surmise that it was the common stock of shared belief in the much larger Christian community, at a time considerably prior to Paul's writing of this letter.

2 TIMOTHY 1:9–10

This grace was given us in Christ Jesus before the beginning of time, but it has now been revealed through the appearing of our Savior, Christ

Jesus, who has destroyed death and has brought life and immortality to light through the gospel.

Even though the impoverishment motif does not occur in 2 Timothy 1:9–10, this passage does emphasize Christ's redeeming work.[1] And once more Christ's preexistence and the genuineness of his incarnation is presupposed. Christ's preexistence is asserted by the clause "which was given to us *in Christ Jesus before the ages began.*" His incarnation is then expressed by the clause "it has now been revealed *through the appearing of our Savior, Christ Jesus.*" This very Pauline concern thus finds expression in the corpus yet one more time. Christ preexisted with the Father, and at one point in human history he became incarnate in order to redeem.

Christ the Son as the Sent One

It is in light of the previously discussed passages that we should read the two "sending" passages in Galatians and Romans. Although some have argued otherwise, both the grammar and the context of these passages call for an incarnational reading of their extraordinary affirmations. Both are set in contexts where Paul's concern is that Christ and the Spirit have made Torah observance obsolete, and both are therefore altogether soteriological, since in each case Paul asserts that God sent his Son to free humankind from enslavement to both Torah and death. We consider each of these passages in turn, followed by a brief discussion of related passages in 1 Timothy.

GALATIANS 4:4–7

But when the set time had fully come, God sent his Son, born of a woman, born under the law, to redeem those under the law, that we might receive adoption to sonship. Because you are his sons, God sent the Spirit of his

---

1. By bringing this passage into the discussion, I am not attempting to argue for or against Pauline authorship of this letter, although I personally lean strongly in its favor. This letter exists in the New Testament because up through the eighteenth century it was believed by the church to have been written by Paul. And the singular reason for bringing it into this discussion is to note that its Christology, despite being expressed in different ways at times, is fully in keeping with Paul.

Son into our hearts, the Spirit who calls out, "*Abba*, Father." So you are
no longer a slave, but God's child.

Galatians 4:4–7 offers the christological-soteriological basis for Paul's
singular interest throughout the letter—that because they are *in Christ*,
the Galatian gentiles absolutely do not need to come *under Torah*. Thus
the passage has been shaped with this singular concern in view. As Paul
argues in a variety of ways throughout his letter, God's "time" came with
Christ, especially through his redemptive work on the cross, followed
by resurrection.

In Galatians 4:4, Paul declares, in language that seems deliberately
chosen to tie together the work of Christ and the Spirit, that "God *sent*
his Son." Two clues indicate that this is an assertion of Christ's preexistence, that the Son is himself divine and was sent from the Father
to effect redemption.

First, although it is true, as some have argued, that the verb Paul uses
for "sent" does not necessarily imply the sending forth of a preexistent
being, the verb is not used here in isolation. The overall evidence of the
passage points in the direction of preexistence. The verb *may* refer to
sending forth a heavenly being, and the overall context and language
of this passage, especially the verb's occurrence in a crucial clause in
Galatians 4:6, suggests that it *does* indeed do so here. This is confirmed
by the fact that Paul begins his next sentence by saying exactly the same
thing about the Spirit. Using language reminiscent of a significant
moment in the Psalter (Ps. 104:30), and in a clause that is both parallel
with and intimately related to what he said in his opening two clauses
(Gal. 4:4–5), Paul says that "God sent forth *the Spirit of his Son* into
our hearts" with the *Abba*-cry (v. 6).[2] In so doing the Apostle thus veri-
fies that our sonship is secured by the Son whom God had previously
"sent." The parallelism between the sending of the Son and the sending
of the Spirit—which can refer only to the preexistence of *the Spirit of
God*, now understood equally as the Spirit of the Son—confirms that
in the first instance Paul is speaking presuppositionally about Christ's
preexistence. As F. F. Bruce once pointed out, "If the Spirit was the

2. See chap. 7 below, which discusses the *Abba*-cry in more detail.

Spirit before God sent him, the Son was presumably the Son before God sent *him*."[3]

Second, in keeping with his whole argument to this point, Paul writes of the work of Christ as an objective, historical reality. At God's own set time Christ entered our human history ("born of a woman") within the context of God's own people ("born under the law") so as to free people from Torah observance by giving them "adoption to sonship" (Gal. 4:4–5). The otherwise unnecessary phrase "born of a woman" should catch the reader's attention. How else, one might ask, could a human be brought into the world? Although Paul's primary concern here lies with the next two phrases—"born under the law, to redeem those under the law"—his mention of Christ as "born of a woman" only makes sense if Christ's preexistence is the presupposition of the whole sentence. Paul's point here—made in passing though it seems to be—is that Christ is the incarnate one, the one who thereby stands in stark contrast to the ahistorical, atemporal, "elemental spiritual forces of the world" (v. 3) to which these former pagans had been subject.

ROMANS 8:2–4

Through Jesus Christ the law of the Spirit who gives life has set you free from the law of sin and death. For what the law was powerless to do because it was weakened by the flesh, God did by sending his own Son in the likeness of sinful flesh to be a sin offering. And so he condemned sin in the flesh, in order that the righteous requirement of the law might be fully met in us, who do not live according to the flesh but according to the Spirit.

In a sentence that at once both picks up the preceding argumentation regarding the relationship of the law and sin (Rom. 7:4–6) and concludes the lengthy digression over the question of whether Torah itself is evil, Paul sets out to elaborate "the law of the Spirit" noted at the end of his opening sentence (8:2; cf. 7:22–23). The reality of the Spirit who gives life is itself predicated on the redemptive work of Christ. Thus, in referring to Christ's role in making Torah observance obsolete, Paul speaks once more in terms of God sending the Son to redeem, and Paul does

---

3. F. F. Bruce, *Commentary on Galatians* (Grand Rapids: Eerdmans, 1982), 195.

so in language reminiscent of his prior affirmation of this reality in Galatians 4:4–5.

But in Romans 8 the Apostle speaks of the work of Christ in terms of God's having thus "condemned sin in the flesh" (v. 3), which is almost certainly a piece of double entendre: that in Christ's own death "in the [literal] flesh" God condemned the sin that resides in our "flesh," that is, our fallen nature. Paul's explanation of how God did this is provided in the central modifier, "by sending his own Son in the likeness of sinful flesh to be a sin offering" (v. 3), which can mean only that Christ assumed genuine humanity but did so without yielding to sin.

As we have observed repeatedly on the matter of Christ's preexistence and incarnation, Paul neither argues for them nor presents them as essential to his present point; instead, these two realities are the natural presupposition of Paul's language, especially the language of God "*sending his own* Son in the likeness of sinful flesh." These phrases—especially in light of the passages we have already examined—clearly assume that Christ had not experienced "flesh" before he was sent. What should catch the eye in this instance is the unique phrase "his *own* Son" in which "his own" is in the emphatic middle position in Paul's Greek phrase. This is hardly the language of "adoption"; to the contrary, it assumes the unique relationship with the Father that is the prerogative only of the Son, while at the same time it anticipates the allusion to Abraham and Isaac that will appear a bit later (Rom. 8:32).

Furthermore, the phrase "in the likeness of sinful flesh," as with the phrase "in human likeness" in Philippians 2:7, means that Jesus was similar to our "flesh" in some respects but dissimilar in others. Paul's use of the word "flesh" indicates his intention since if Paul intended a more complete identification with us in our sinfulness itself, he could easily have said simply "in sinfulness," that is, in our fallen human condition. So in this case not only are Christ's preexistence and incarnation presupposed by what Paul says but so also is Christ's sinlessness—even if Paul's ultimate concern here lies with Christ's genuine humanity.

1 TIMOTHY 1:15

Here is a trustworthy saying that deserves full acceptance: Christ Jesus came into the world to save sinners—of whom I am the worst.

1 TIMOTHY 2:5

For there is one God and one mediator between God and mankind, the man Christ Jesus.

1 TIMOTHY 3:16

He appeared in the flesh, was vindicated by the Spirit, was seen by angels.

In 1 Timothy 1:15 the "trustworthy saying" changes the focus slightly from Christ having been "sent," though the point remains: "Christ Jesus came into the world to save sinners." As with the preceding passages we have discussed, this sentence does not *require* that preexistence is in view. Nevertheless, this phrase is a strange way of referring to Christ's redemptive death if it does not presuppose preexistence. A more creedal way to make the point, as Paul does in 1 Corinthians 15:3, would be to say simply that Christ Jesus "died" to save sinners.

The emphasis on Christ's coming into the world in this passage is reiterated in the two succeeding moments in 1 Timothy (2:5 and 3:16) with specific interest in the reality of the incarnation, which reinforce an incarnational reading of 1:15. The work of the one mediator between God and humanity was accomplished by one who was himself fully human (2:5). Such an assertion implies both preexistence and incarnation. And such a view of these first two affirmations is confirmed by the first line in the poetry of the final passage, that "he appeared [lit., was *manifested*] in the flesh" (3:16). Indeed, this emphasis is almost certainly in response to a kind of latent Docetism in the negation of the material world that is being refuted in this letter.

Conclusion

So what is one to make of this evidence that Paul and his churches held in common the conviction that their Savior, the Lord, Jesus Christ, had preexisted as God's Son and had been "sent" into the world to effect redemption? How does this reality affect our overall understanding of Paul's Christology?

First, Paul clearly understood Christ the Savior to be himself divine and not simply a divine *agent*. If most of Paul's christological emphases have to do with Christ's present postresurrection reign as Lord, the Pauline passages examined above make it clear that in Christ's coming, "God was pleased to have all his fullness dwell" in the human Jesus Christ (Col. 1:19). Thus the full deity of Christ is never something Paul argues for; rather, as we have noted throughout, it is the constant presupposition of everything he says about Christ as Savior. And surely this presupposed reality accounts in large measure for Paul's Christ devotion, examined in chapter 1. To be sure, Paul only rarely speaks as he does in Galatians 2:20 of "the Son of God, who loved me and gave himself for me," but the very fact that in this case he purposely identifies Christ as "the Son of God" suggests that what overwhelms Paul about such love is not simply Christ's death on his behalf. What lies behind such wonder is Paul's overwhelming sense that the preexistent, and therefore divine, Son of God is the one who through his incarnation and crucifixion "gave himself for me." The deity of Christ is therefore no small matter for Paul; it is of central significance to his understanding of, and devotion to, his Lord.

Second, there is, especially in Paul's later letters, a considerable emphasis on Christ's genuine humanity, which complements Paul's conviction about Christ's true identity as the divine Son. The emphasis on Christ's genuine humanity in Paul's later letters suggests that by this time—a full generation after the death and resurrection of Christ—Paul already has to fight on a second front, namely, against those whose understanding of Christ's *deity* might minimize the reality of Christ's *humanity*. While none of these passages is overtly antidocetic, they nonetheless either speak to or anticipate the heresy of Docetism. Paul will have none of such heretical nonsense. By saying that Christ came "in human likeness" or "in the likeness of sinful flesh," Paul does not mean that Christ's flesh was not real (bodily) flesh like ours. Rather, his language safeguards both dimensions of a genuine incarnation: that in Christ one who was truly God lived a truly human life.

The twofold emphasis on Christ's divinity and humanity is the assumed Christology that lies behind Paul's statements examined in this chapter. At the same time, we must hold these statements of Christ's divinity together with Paul's insistence elsewhere that there is only *one* Lord, *one* Spirit, and *one* God (Eph. 4:4–6; cf. 1 Cor. 12:4–6), along with Paul's repeated emphasis on the divine triad as responsible for our salvation. After all, it is precisely these very early affirmations and emphases that caused the early church to work through how best to express the conviction that there is ever and only but one God but that the one God must be understood to include Father, Son, and Spirit. Indeed, as we examine more closely in the concluding chapter, these passages in Paul—along with similar affirmations in the Johannine corpus and the book of Hebrews—demand that the church try to articulate how the One God was in fact "Three in One."

PART 2

The Second Adam

In the conclusion to chapter 2, it was noted that in some of Paul's later letters he appears to move toward an emphasis on Christ's humanity when speaking of the incarnation. Throughout the centuries, however, Christianity has not always fared well on this point and has frequently veered in the direction of a fourth-century heresy known as Apollinarianism. Here the church pays lip service to Christ's humanity but often emphasizes his deity in ways that downplay the genuineness of that humanity. Thus a fourth-century bishop named Apollinaris affirmed that Christ had a fully human body, but he argued that it was inhabited by a divine mind. This view was ultimately rejected by the orthodox church for eliminating the genuine humanity of Christ—since Jesus's divine mind, even as a child, would not have had to develop and learn as the human mind must. Unfortunately, the influence of this unbiblical heresy can still be felt at times in the church today.

In part 2, then, we pursue the affirmation of Christ's genuine humanity in the Pauline letters by turning our attention to Paul's references, and in some cases apparent allusions, to Christ as second or last "Adam." To be sure, there is disagreement over how much in Paul's letters should be included in such a discussion, since Adam is specifically mentioned only three times (1 Cor. 15:21–22, 44–49; Rom. 5:12–21). Rather than focusing narrowly on Paul's use of the name Adam, the discussion is broadened to include the Apostle's use of related imagery from the creation narrative in Genesis, including Paul's language of the new creation, the second Adam, and the *imago Dei* (chap. 3). Broadening the discussion in this way allows for a thorough treatment of the topic of Christ's work as the creator of a new creation and new humanity, even though in some instances the allusion to Adam may have been distant. We then turn to Paul's emphasis on the true humanity of the second Adam, Jesus of Nazareth (chap. 4).

3

Paul and New Creation Theology

The point of departure in this chapter is with the term "new creation," which occurs twice in Paul's letters (2 Cor. 5:17; Gal. 6:15), where both instances seem clearly intended to echo the beginning of the Genesis narrative (chaps. 1–3). That is followed by a closer look at the three explicit mentions of Adam in Paul's letters, including an examination of the crucial word *eikōn*, or "image," with reference to Christ, which is likely a reference to Adam as the term is borrowed from the Genesis narrative as it would have appeared in Paul's Greek Bible, the Septuagint.

The New Creation

On three occasions, in letters spanning nearly a decade and in situations aimed toward behavioral change, Paul bases his argument on the fact that with the coming of Christ Jesus, especially as the result of his death and resurrection, God had inaugurated the "new creation" promised toward the end of Isaiah (65:17–25). This usage is in keeping with the "already, but not yet" eschatological framework that characterizes Paul's theology as a whole, which he held in common with the rest of the early church. These early believers had come to understand that Christ, through his death and resurrection, had inaugurated the *beginning* of the end (the "already"), while they still awaited its *consummation* (the "not yet"). Two passages in Paul's letters make this point explicitly, while a third provides more detail without using the actual language itself. Here we consider each passage in turn, beginning with the earliest.

2 CORINTHIANS 5:14–17

For Christ's love compels us, because we are convinced that one died for all, and therefore all died. And he died for all, that those who live should no longer live for themselves but for him who died for them and was raised again. So from now on we regard no one from a worldly point of view. Though we once regarded Christ in this way, we do so no longer. Therefore, if anyone is in Christ, the *new creation* has come: The old has gone, the new is here!

In our first passage, Paul deliberately confronts those in Corinth who have been calling into question both the Apostle's gospel of a crucified Messiah and his own cruciform apostleship. The new creation brought about by Christ's death and resurrection, Paul argues, nullifies the point of view of the old age. The phrase Paul uses here could be translated literally as "according to the flesh," which most likely began as a play on words regarding the circumcision of the male child's sexual organ, but since such a wordplay is no longer readily accessible to readers, especially in English, the NIV translators have rightly rendered it "from a worldly point of view" (2 Cor. 5:16).

From the Apostle's perspective, Christ's death means that the whole human race has come under the sentence of death so that those who have been raised to life (in God's new order) now live for the one "who died for them and was raised again" (2 Cor. 5:15). The result, Paul explains, is that from henceforth to view either Christ or anyone (or anything) from a perspective that is "according to the flesh" is no longer valid. Why? Because being in Christ means that one has become a part of "the new creation," since in Christ "the old has gone, the new is here" (v. 17). This radical new point of view—life marked by the cross and awaiting the resurrection—lies at the heart of, and serves as the basis for, almost everything Paul thinks and does.

GALATIANS 6:14–16

May I never boast except in the cross of our Lord, Jesus Christ, through which the world has been crucified to me, and I to the world. Neither circumcision nor uncircumcision means anything; what counts is the *new creation*. Peace and mercy to all who follow this rule—to the Israel of God.

In his letter to the believers in Galatia, the most singularly passionate letter in the preserved Pauline collection, the Apostle concludes by asserting that the old order that distinguished people on the basis of the rite of circumcision has yielded to the new order. Earlier in this letter (Gal. 3:26–29), Paul stated plainly that participation in Christ's death and resurrection by faith and through baptism had radicalized everything. In the new order neither religious ethnicity (Jew/gentile), nor social status (slave/free), nor gender identity (male/female) counts for anything in terms of one's relationship with God. As his parting words to these believers with whom he was somewhat at odds, he asserts once more that value and privilege based on status had been brought to nothing with the inauguration of the *new creation*.

Paul's point throughout his letter has been that in the new order of things the ground—at the foot of the cross, as it were—is equal. In the present passage, his point is that gentile believers must *not* be coerced to become circumcised, as some were arguing, since in the new order established by Christ's death and resurrection the former identity markers no longer persist. Life in the Spirit has eliminated the need to keep the old order of life under the law.

As a final apposition, Paul offers the most astounding affirmation of all: that those who are part of this new creation are now in fact the "Israel of God" (Gal. 6:16). God has not abandoned his ancient people; rather, both Jew and gentile together are now, in Christ, being re-created into the divine image. Paul's concern is that those who belong to God as children are thus to bear the divine image in their relationships with others. This is why Paul stresses that *behavior* (not "works") that corresponds to that of God and Christ—love for one's enemies, caring for the poor, breaking down ethnic and cultural boundaries (Jew and gentile as *one people* of God)—is so important in the new creation begun through Christ's death and resurrection.

COLOSSIANS 3:8–11

But now you must also rid yourselves of all such things as these: anger, rage, malice, slander, and filthy language from your lips. Do not lie to each other, since you have taken off your old self with its practices and have put on the new self, which is being renewed in knowledge in the image of its Creator. Here there is no Gentile or Jew, circumcised or uncircumcised, barbarian, Scythian, slave or free, but Christ is all, and is in all.

With the preceding two passages as background, the significance of Colossians 3:8–11 can be appreciated. Although this passage lacks the term "new creation," it suggests as much when it speaks of "the new self" as "being renewed in knowledge in the image of its Creator" (v. 10). We examine Paul's use of the word *eikōn* at greater length in the final section of this chapter. For now we simply note Paul's emphasis on Christ as the absolute focal point of the new creation.

Earlier in the letter, Paul asserted that entrance into the new humanity is by way of Christ's death and resurrection, understood to be evidenced by Colossian believers having been united with Christ in baptism (Col. 2:12). Now he reiterates the radical new order that emerges as a result—a new order in which all merely human-based distinctions predicated on ethnicity (no gentile or Jew), religion (circumcised or uncircumcised), cultural status (barbarian, Scythian), or social status (slave or free) are abolished (echoing his earlier statement in Gal. 3:28). As important as these distinctions would have been to most people in their everyday lives in the Roman Empire—and continue to be in many cultures today—Paul insists that they have no significance of any kind in terms of one's *relationship with God* and thus no impact on everyday relationships within the community of faith.

In this passage Paul echoes language used in the narrative of the creation of Adam and Eve (Gen. 1:26–27; cf. 9:6) as well as phrases from the Christ-poem with which the letter began (Col. 1:15, 18). Significantly, everything in this letter as a whole, and in this passage in particular, indicates that the creator is Christ himself. Christ alone is in view in both the immediate context of the passage and the broader context (2:20–3:11). Moreover, in the opening Christ-hymn (1:15–20), Christ is both the divine image bearer and the one through whom the original creation came to be. Likewise, he is called the *archē* ("beginning") of the new creation (1:18).

Thus the one who as the Son of God bears the divine image is also the one who by virtue of his death and resurrection is now re-creating a people into that same image. This passage thus reinforces the new creation motif by use of the language of the divine image. This combination of ideas and language lays the christological groundwork for understanding Paul's discussions of Christ as the second Adam.

The Second Adam

All three of the explicit comparisons between Christ and Adam occur in contexts where Christ's humanity is in full view as the presupposition behind Paul's concern, even if it is not necessarily his emphasis. At issue in all three of these comparisons are the two basic realities of our humanity: sin and death, which Adam let loose in our humanity and which Christ as second Adam overcame by his death and resurrection. Two of these comparisons are found in the same chapter, 1 Corinthians 15, and the third is found in Romans 5.

1 CORINTHIANS 15:21–22

For since death came through a man, the resurrection of the dead comes also through a man. For as in Adam all die, so in Christ all will be made alive.

Paul says nothing in 1 Corinthians—or in his two earliest letters (1 and 2 Thessalonians)—to prepare one for the sudden mention of Adam in 1 Corinthians 15. It appears near the beginning of the second phase of Paul's threefold argument with the Corinthians over the matter of the future *bodily* resurrection of believers, regarding which some of the Corinthians are less than keen! Paul first presents Christ's own resurrection as the basis of ours (1 Cor. 15:1–11), then spells out in detail the *necessity* of Christ's resurrection (vv. 12–34), and finally indicates something of the *nature* of a body that has been raised and adapted to life in eternity (vv. 35–58). That he does this again in much the same matter-of-fact way in his later letter to the believers in Rome (Rom. 5) suggests that he had previously reflected on this analogy before it appears here for the first time in the extant letters.

In this first instance the analogy is simple and straightforward: death became a human reality because of the first *anthrōpos* ("human"), Adam; similarly, resurrection will become a future reality for believers because of the resurrection of the second *anthrōpos*, Christ Jesus. This is then repeated with emphasis on its effects for other humans: "as in Adam all die, so in Christ all will be made alive" (1 Cor. 15:22). Since this is in direct response to a denial by some Corinthians of a future bodily resurrection of believers, the emphasis is altogether on the fact that, just as the *anthrōpos* who stands at the beginning of the old creation brought death into the world, so also the *anthrōpos* who stands at the beginning of the new creation has, through his death (and resurrection), secured a future bodily resurrection for those who are his.

1 CORINTHIANS 15:44–49

If there is a natural body, there is also a spiritual body. So it is written: "The first man Adam became a living being";[1] the last Adam, a life-giving spirit. The spiritual did not come first, but the natural, and after that the spiritual. The first man was of the dust of the earth; the second man is of heaven. As was the earthly man, so are those who are of the earth; and as is the heavenly man, so also are those who are of heaven. And just as we have borne the image of the earthly man, so let us[2] bear the image of the heavenly man.

The emphasis in Paul's second use of the Adam-Christ analogy in 1 Corinthians 15 is once again on the fact that Christ is the last *anthrōpos*, but in this case the analogy becomes a bit more complex because the issue has changed considerably. In the first two sections of this long argument (1 Cor. 15:1–11 and 12–34), the focus had been on the reality of the *future* resurrection of believers, which is predicated on Christ's own resurrection. The focus in the third phase of the argument (vv. 35–49) is on the *bodily nature* of that future resurrection. And if from our later perspective Paul goes at this in a somewhat prolix way, it is almost surely because he is intent on emphasizing that the *risen* Christ continues to have a body that is related to his life as a human. Paul does this by way

1. Gen. 2:7.
2. I am providing the NIV marginal reading here, which is almost certainly Paul's original, since it appears in all but one of the early and best manuscripts.

of the adjectives *psychikos* and *pneumatikos*, which in this case mean something like "natural" and "supernatural," respectively—usage that is probably intended to be somewhat ironic since the Corinthians apparently disdained *psychikos* human bodies. So by way of these two adjectives, Paul argues that the body that Christ Jesus bore in his incarnation was very much the same as the one we all bear, thus fully and completely adapted to earthly life. But the body that he has come to bear by way of resurrection has been refitted for the final life of the Spirit. Thus it is the same body, yet it is not quite the same. The various complexities of this part of Paul's argument are all related to this phenomenon.

The result is that the first *anthrōpos*, Adam, had a body that was of the earth and made of earthly stuff ("the dust of the earth," 1 Cor. 15:47). The second *anthrōpos*, while once having borne this earthly body, now has the same body as it is fitted for heaven ("of heaven," v. 47). The reason for this somewhat complex way of saying it turns out to be a matter of exhortation. Paul wants the Corinthians to live in such a way that they will be among those who at the resurrection will also bear the "image" of the second Adam since they do indeed already bear the "image" of the first Adam (v. 49).

Even though most English versions render the verb in 1 Corinthians 15:49 as a future indicative ("so we shall"; Gk. short "o"), the superior manuscript evidence makes it quite clear that Paul himself wrote to the Corinthians in the imperative ("so *let us*"; Gk. long "o"), meaning that they should do so now in the present age. Paul's point is plain, especially in light of all that has preceded till now: if we bear Christ's *name* in the present, we must also bear his *likeness* in our relationships with one another and with the world.

To be sure, the direction of the argument in this case has changed a bit; nonetheless, Paul's emphasis on Christ's having been "truly human" continues from before. The difference is that Christ is now spoken of as the progenitor of the *new* humanity, just as Adam has been of the *first*. Thus in both instances of this analogy where Paul is challenging the Corinthians' tacit denial of a future *bodily* resurrection, his concern is singular: Christ in his humanity, through death and resurrection, has not simply identified with us as humans but has set a future resurrection in motion—as a new creation with its eventual realization of a new body, fully adapted to the life of the future. And the basis for all of this is the historical reality that in his incarnation Christ bore a body that was truly in keeping with that of Adam.

ROMANS 5:12–21

Therefore, just as sin entered the world through one man [*anthrōpos*], and death through sin, and in this way death came to all people [*anthrōpoi*] . . . how much more did God's grace and the gift that came by the grace of the one man [*anthrōpos*], Jesus Christ, overflow to the many! . . . For just as through the disobedience of the one man [*anthrōpos*] the many were made sinners, so also through the obedience of the one man [*anthrōpos*] the many will be made righteous.

The concern in both instances of the Adam-Christ contrast in 1 Corinthians 15 had to do with death and life as such. When Paul returns to this analogy at the beginning of the second step in his presentation of the gospel to the believers in Rome (Rom. 5:12–8:29), his central concern is still on death and life. The issue now, however, is not death itself but the cause of death, sin. Despite the focus on sin and righteousness that leads to his use of the Adam-Christ analogy—a focus that is repeated throughout and follows from it—Paul continues with this analogy to emphasize death and life. What Adam let loose in the world was sin, which led to death; what Christ brought into the world was righteousness, which leads to life. And, as with 1 Corinthians 15, throughout Paul's argument in Romans 5 he repeatedly uses *anthrōpos* for both Adam and Christ.

All three explicit mentions of Adam and Christ in the extant Pauline corpus are narrowly focused; in each case the analogy has specifically to do with the one being responsible for bringing death into the world, through his sin, and the other being responsible for bringing life into the world through his death and resurrection. But nothing more is made of the analogy. Hence one can understand why many take a minimalist position on this matter. Paul's point in using the analogy seems plain, especially in light of all that has preceded up to this point. And if one stays only with what these few affirmations say specifically, there is hardly ground for such a thing as an "Adam Christology." But something more does need to be said of these three affirmations, because in each case there is considerable emphasis on Adam and Christ as standing at the *beginning of something*. For Paul they are the progenitors of the two creations, a fallen one that has issued in sin and death and a new one that has been issued in by crucifixion and resurrection. But if an Adam Christology is only implicit in the analogy in the passages we have just considered, it is made explicit in Paul's several discussions of the divine image, to which we now turn.

The Image of God

In light of the new creation and second Adam passages examined above, there is good reason to believe that Paul's several references to the Son of God as bearing the divine "image" (Gk. *eikōn*) are intentionally contrasting Adam with Christ (as the second Adam). This seems especially so since Paul's first use of *eikōn* in this way is in the immediate context of his analogy of Adam and Christ discussed above (1 Cor. 15:49).

What is less clear in the scholarly literature is where one places the emphasis on Paul's use of the word *eikōn*—whether it is on Christ's *bearing* the divine image or on his *replacing* Adam as the one true human in whom the divine image has been restored. Or perhaps Paul's emphasis is somewhat (deliberately?) ambiguous. In an attempt to answer this question, we consider several passages that use the term *eikōn*. We treat them according to their likely chronological order, since we can learn something by doing so.

1 Corinthians 15:49

And just as we have borne the image of the earthly man, so let us[3] bear the *image* of the heavenly man.

First Corinthians 15:49 provides the earliest use of *eikōn* in the Pauline corpus. As we saw above, Paul's concern in this passage is to help the Corinthians understand the future *bodily* resurrection of believers (1 Cor. 15:35–49), and he tries to accomplish this by returning to the analogy

---

3. Again, I am providing the NIV marginal reading here. See note 2 above.

between Adam and Christ introduced earlier (vv. 21–22), which echoes the opening narrative of the Bible (Gen. 1). With what appears to be a kind of double entendre, Paul's emphasis lies first on the bodily nature of the resurrection, which Christ now bears and which all who are in Christ will eventually bear. But, second, Paul cannot keep himself from urging them to live in the present with that future in view.

Thus in this moment near the end of the letter, Paul emphasizes Christ's bearing the image of God, or *imago Dei*, in his human life, even if the purpose of his argument is to describe Christ's truly human, but now transformed, body. There is no emphasis on Christ's deity as such; rather, in his coming as the second Adam, Christ did what Adam failed to do: to bear the divine image *in his humanity* and thus to serve as the progenitor of all others who, by means of the Spirit, are to do the same.

2 CORINTHIANS 3:18

And we all, who with unveiled faces contemplate the Lord's glory, are being transformed into his *image* with ever-increasing glory, which comes from the Lord, who is the Spirit.

2 CORINTHIANS 4:4–6

The god of this age has blinded the minds of unbelievers, so that they cannot see the light of the gospel that displays the glory of Christ, who is the *image* of God. For what we preach is not ourselves, but Jesus Christ as Lord, and ourselves as your servants for Jesus' sake. For God, who said, "Let light shine out of darkness,"[4] made his light shine in our hearts to give us the light of the knowledge of God's glory displayed in the face of Christ.

The most striking thing about the set of affirmations in 2 Corinthians 3 and 4 is that the first appearance of *eikōn* (3:18) is generated not by the passage from Genesis but by the mirror imagery that Paul uses in writing to believers in a city famous for its bronze mirrors. But if this comparison is used to catch their attention, which was very likely Paul's intent, the main thrust of the sentence has to do with Christ bearing the unfading divine glory (in contrast to the fading glory that Moses experienced). Paul's point for his Corinthian audience is that as they

4. Gen. 1:3.

by the Spirit gaze on Christ as into a mirror, they are themselves being transformed into that same "image," the image of God that has been borne fully and perfectly by Christ.

When in the next phase of the argument Paul returns to the twofold language of "image" and "glory" (2 Cor. 4:4), the focus is now on Christ. The emphasis in this second instance is not primarily on Christ's humanity as such—that is assumed as inherent in the imagery itself—but is on the true image of God being borne by the one *who shares the divine glory*, the one who, when turned to in devotion and obedience, by his Spirit transforms believers into the image of God that humanity was created for in the first place. But even with this different emphasis, the use of this language for Christ presupposes his humanity, which is the only reason for such language being used of Christ at all.

We have seen two places in the extant Corinthian correspondence where Paul uses the language of the opening narrative of the Bible (Gen. 1) with reference to Christ. In the first instance, his central concern is with Christ's bearing the image *in his humanity* (1 Cor. 15:49); in the second, the emphasis is on the same Christ sharing the *divine glory* with the Father (2 Cor. 4:4–6). Thus Christ is the one human who, because he is fully divine, bears the perfect image of God—the image into which believers themselves are in the process of being conformed.

ROMANS 8:29

For those God foreknew he also predestined to be conformed to the *image* of his Son, that he might be the firstborn among many brothers and sisters.

With the explanatory sentence in Romans 8:29, one comes to the first of the two *eikōn* passages (with Col. 1:15, discussed below) where Christ is explicitly referred to as the "Son" of the Father. In both instances the two-sided reality (human and divine) is a play on the language from the beginning of the whole biblical narrative (Gen. 1), and in both cases Paul also refers to the Son as God's *prōtotokos* ("firstborn"), a word that is never used of Adam in any of the Jewish literature. By using this term, Paul is not speaking of temporality, as if Christ were the first in a series, but of the one who holds all the *rights* of primogeniture. Thus even though an Adam Christology likely lies behind the language in both instances, the emphasis seems not to lie there but to be moving toward a messianic Son of God Christology.

The appearance of this combination of *eikōn* and *prōtotokos* in the present passage comes as the climactic moment in Paul's elaboration of what living in and by the Spirit looks like (Rom. 8:1–30). His goal is to assure the believers in Rome, both Jew and gentile together as one people of God, of the work of Christ on their behalf and of God's gift of the Spirit—the Spirit of both the Father and the Son (8:9–10). Thus the Spirit is for them both the enabler of ethical life now and the guarantor of eternal life to come.

Thus in a sentence that begins on the double note of God's foreknowing and predestining them, Paul interrupts his sentence to spell out the shape and the ultimate goal of that predestination. God has foreordained not that they make it to heaven, as it were, but that in the present they be "conformed to the image of his Son," who himself is God's "firstborn" among the many who are to become his "brothers and sisters."

Deeply embedded in such language is a twofold emphasis: first, that the eternal Son of God perfectly bears the divine image and, second, that he does so in his identity with us in our humanity. This first emphasis is almost immediately picked up when Paul—with an echo of a crucial moment in the Abraham narrative (Gen. 22)—refers to the crucifixion by asserting that God "did not spare *his own* Son" but gave him up for our sakes (Rom. 8:32). The second emphasis, on Christ's humanity, is contained within verse 29 itself, with the phrase "the firstborn among many brothers and sisters." Even though there is no direct echo of the opening chapter of Genesis in this passage (though the allusion to Abraham takes us back to the Genesis narrative), it would seem fair to conclude that where Adam failed as God's "firstborn," Christ has succeeded—something foreordained by God from eternity past.

Colossians 1:15

The Son is the *image* of the invisible God, the firstborn over all creation.

The remarkable word about our Savior in Colossians 1:15 is the first of two such affirmations about Christ that have a poetic, almost hymnic, ring to them. Both strophes of this Christ-poem (Col. 1:15–17 and 18–20) make sense precisely as one takes seriously that "the Son [God] loves" (v. 13) is the grammatical subject governing both the beginning of the first stanza (v. 15) and the beginning of the second stanza (v. 18). Thus Paul is here echoing what he said to the believers in Rome (Rom. 8:29, discussed above) but with considerably different concerns.

These new concerns are to identify the Son as the *messianic* Son of God (Col. 1:13), which seems to be confirmed in verse 15 by his addition that the Son is also the Father's *prōtotokos*, thus echoing what came to be understood as a messianic passage from the Psalter (Ps. 89:26–27). Paul also affirms that "the Son" has the rights of primogeniture with regard to the whole of creation—which also came into existence through him. Thus Paul's emphasis with his use of *eikōn* in this passage is on the incarnate Son of God as the *divine* image bearer, who in eternity past was both the agent and the goal of the created order.

That Paul is here once again (indirectly, but surely deliberately) echoing the original creation narrative (Gen. 1) is confirmed by the way he begins the second strophe of the poem by stating that the Son is the *archē* ("beginning"). This most unusual language is a direct echo of the first words of the Bible (Gen. 1:1), and as with the term *eikōn* that begins the first strophe, the term *archē* is immediately followed by a second use of *prōtotokos*. But now the referent is to Christ's being the "firstborn" of the *new* creation, marked by his resurrection from the dead. Thus even though the word *eikōn* does not occur in the second strophe (Col. 1:18–20), it is assumed throughout, so that the emphasis on the Son's bearing the *divine* image in the first strophe moves toward his identity with us in his bringing about reconciliation in the second strophe. The One in whom all the divine fullness dwells bodily has brought the reconciliation through the blood of his cross (vv. 19–20), which leads us to the sixth instance in which Paul uses *eikōn* with regard to Christ.

Colossians 3:10

[You] have put on the new self, which is being renewed in knowledge in the *image* of its Creator.

With the remarkable assertion in Colossians 3:10, the concerns of the present chapter are brought full circle. Having earlier identified Christ as the bearer of the divine *eikōn* (1:15), Paul now adds that the new person is "being renewed" (= re-created) in keeping with the *eikōn* of him who has created the new person. Thus as creator of the first Adam, Christ now functions as the re-creator of the new humanity, the ultimate goal of which is re-creation into his *own* image and thus into the divine image. Thus the one who re-creates broken and fallen humanity back into the divine image is none other than the one who is himself the "image" of God—the Father's own "firstborn," the one who by virtue of his resurrection is the "firstborn" with regard to the new creation. The creator of the first creation, who himself bears the Father's image, is now seen as the creator of the new creation, as he restores his own people back into the divine image and thus into his own image that he alone perfectly bears. Here the emphasis is simultaneously on Christ as the *divine* image-bearer and on Christ as the one who now re-creates fallen *humanity* into that same image.

Philippians 2:6–8

Who, being in very nature God, did not consider equality with God something to be used to his own advantage; rather, he made himself nothing by taking the very nature of a servant, being made in human likeness. And being found in appearance as a man, he humbled himself by becoming obedient to death—even death on a cross.

We examined Philippians 2:6–8 in chapter 2, and we return to it here at the end of this analysis of Paul's use of *eikōn* because there has been a veritable groundswell in the New Testament academy that has argued (or more often simply asserted) that Paul's use of *morphē* (NIV "nature") in the opening phrase of the Christ story (v. 6) is virtually synonymous with *eikōn*. But this is a piece of scholarly mythology that needs to be laid to rest! The preceding discussion of Paul's use of the term *eikōn* allows us to see this, while at the same time demonstrating that the presupposition of the phrase "in the form" nevertheless reinforces Christ's preincarnate divine existence.

There are two reasons for rejecting the view that *morphē* is virtually synonymous with *eikōn*. First, as noted earlier, Paul's apparent reason for choosing the term *morphē* is that it was the only word available in the

Greek language that could serve equally well to define Christ's mode of preexistence with God and to indicate the extreme nature of the mode of his incarnation—coming into our history in the "nature," or "form," of a slave.[5]

Second, Paul's use of *eikōn* elsewhere in his letters demonstrates both the folly of equating *eikōn* with *morphē* and that, whatever echo the next phrase—about Christ not using his equality with God "to his own advantage"—has with reference to Adam, it cannot include the phrase "in very nature [*morphē*] God" that has preceded. Paul did not intend to begin this poem by saying that Christ was in the image of God with regard to his *preexistent* divine nature, which would border on theological nonsense. As we have seen in the previous passages that use *eikōn*, Paul uses this language with regard to Christ only with reference to his being the divine image-bearer *in his incarnation*, not with regard to his preexistence. This is especially so since this language would make no sense as an echo of the first two chapters of Genesis. Whatever Adam-echo one might find in this grand telling of the story in Philippians 2 is altogether conceptual (in this case, invented by later readers). It lacks a single linguistic tie that could possibly clue the Philippian believers in to such a comparison, if this were Paul's intention. And what the believers in Philippi could neither have heard nor understood can hardly be what Paul intended with this word *morphē*.

Conclusion

In this chapter, we have seen three ways that Paul develops what might be called Adam Christology: first, in Paul's use of "new creation" language; second, in Paul's comparisons and contrasts between Christ and Adam, where Christ is seen as the progenitor of this new creation, who has overturned the effects of Adam's sin that led to death; and, third, in Paul's uses of the term *eikōn*, where the incarnate Christ is seen as the

5. Paul's use of the word "slave" is difficult for modern English-speaking North Americans, whose terrible history of capture and enslavement of native Africans is an eternal blot on our history. But in Paul's first-century context, this language could refer simply to one in a household who, for a variety of reasons, belongs to the owner and thus lacks many of the rights of personal choice.

true bearer of the divine image who is also re-creating a people who are to bear that image with him. These, however, are not the only ways Paul refers to the earthly Jesus. In chapter 4, we turn to an examination of further evidence from Paul's letters where he asserts, and sometimes emphasizes, Christ's true humanity.

4

The Pauline Emphasis

A Truly Human Divine Savior

Throughout the twentieth century, there was considerable debate in New Testament studies regarding Paul's knowledge of, and views about, the historical Jesus of Nazareth. On one extreme was skepticism that Paul had any knowledge of the historical Jesus at all, except for his death by crucifixion. On the other extreme was the idea that Paul viewed Christ almost exclusively in human terms and thought of Christ's "divine" status in terms of a human savior exalted to heaven because of his self-sacrificial death.

In some ways both of these extremes can be seen as a reaction to an earlier Christian orthodoxy that failed to take Jesus's full humanity with genuine seriousness, an orthodoxy that had come to believe on theological grounds that Jesus in his earthly life was *non posse peccare* ("not able to sin"). Such a view must be resisted since ultimately it turns Christ into a divine robot rather than a truly human person who was *posse non peccare* because, using Luke's language, "the grace of God was on him" (Luke 2:40). At issue for this kind of orthodoxy was to build a convincing case for Christ's true humanity that did not look as though his human temptations were not possible for him to act on.

When turning to the apostle Paul with these later theological questions in mind, the most striking thing we observe is the considerable paucity of the data, paucity that is related to the larger issue involved. As we have seen in previous chapters, Paul nowhere tries to *establish* a Christology as such. Rather, because he is primarily dealing with a variety of *behavioral* issues in his churches that need correcting—and need good theology as the way of doing so—his references to Christ are either soteriological in focus or emphasize Christ's present reign as Lord. Nonetheless, Paul drops the curtain just often enough for us to reconstruct what he and his churches believed about Christ—that he was the truly divine Savior who effected salvation through an incarnation in which he became a truly human person. In this chapter we gather these various data points to present a picture of Paul's presuppositional understanding of Christ's humanity.

It is not our purpose to argue the case that Paul had knowledge about the historical Jesus. The evidence for that is clear enough in the passages we examine below. Instead, our goal is simply to present various places in Paul's letters that confirm that he at least knew the traditions about Jesus that are found in the Gospels. Given this evidence, we can see how the *human life* of Jesus was presupposed by everything else that Paul came to believe regarding Jesus's death and resurrection. It is simply unthinkable that in a basically oral and aural culture information about Jesus would not have circulated in a number of ways that would have given the learned Paul knowledge about Jesus's life and teachings. And the evidence suggests that Paul did indeed have knowledge of the historical Jesus. Below we examine the Pauline data under three headings: knowledge of the life of Jesus; knowledge of the teaching of Jesus; and further knowledge of the historical Jesus.

Knowledge of the Life of Jesus

Though relatively few, the pieces of evidence that Paul knew the basic details of the life of Jesus are significant because in each instance the knowledge that Paul seems to assume is incidental to the argument he is making, which makes it all the more trustworthy. As is Paul's pattern when communicating with fellow believers, his statements about the life of Jesus are expressed in such an off-the-cuff way that, at least in some cases, we can assume that his knowledge of Jesus's life was shared by his readers and was therefore not something he had to demonstrate as true. We can see at least four unique aspects of Jesus's life assumed in Paul's letters: that Jesus was considered to be the Jewish Messiah, that he was crucified and raised from the dead, that he was the brother to leaders in the early church and son of Mary, and that his life presented a moral example for Paul and his readers to emulate.

Jewish Messiah

In Paul's argument with the believers in Galatia that they did not need to observe the law, Paul offers a brief account of the life of Jesus that begins with the observation that Jesus was born into an observant Jewish family. Paul writes that when God "sent his Son," this divine Son was "born of a woman, born under the law" (Gal. 4:4). Paul elsewhere notes that Jesus not only was Jewish but also was believed to have been the long-awaited Jewish Messiah (Rom. 9:5; 1:2–4; 1 Cor. 1:22), which further meant that Jesus had come to reign in God's eschatological kingdom (1 Cor. 15:24; Col. 1:13–14). Indeed, Paul's repeated emphasis on Jesus's death and resurrection can best be explained in light of the radical departure of these events from the Jewish messianic expectations—to the extent that its true nature could have been revealed only by the Spirit (1 Cor. 1:20–25; 2:6–10).

Crucified and Resurrected

The historical reality that Jesus died not by stoning (the Jewish way of execution) but by crucifixion (and thus by Roman hands) is writ large in the Pauline corpus. In Paul's earliest preserved letter, he describes Jesus's death as belonging to, and in keeping with, the tradition of the killing of "the prophets" (1 Thess. 2:15). And Paul's earlier allusion to Jesus's sufferings, in the context of the Thessalonians' "severe suffering" (1:6), likely refers not solely to Jesus's crucifixion but also to the beatings and humiliation that preceded it. In light of these early allusions, there is no good reason to doubt the thoroughly Pauline nature of the historical affirmation expressed in a much later letter, which provides the added detail that Jesus made a "good confession" "while testifying before Pontius Pilate" (1 Tim. 6:13).

While it is true that Paul focuses primarily on Jesus's death and resurrection for the purposes of his arguments and exhortations, this says nothing about Paul's further knowledge of the life of Jesus. Paul was addressing particular needs of first-century churches and not writing to satisfy our curiosities. With the exception of his letter (of introduction?) to the believers in Rome, Paul wrote to his own churches for *their* correction or encouragement, not to spell out for later times what knowledge he and his readers held in common.

Brother to Early Church Leaders

A great deal of further knowledge can be assumed to lie behind Paul's passing comments about Jesus's biological brothers who were well-known members of the earliest Jewish Christian community (1 Cor. 9:5; Gal. 1:19). These comments provide intriguing reminders to us of how little we really do know about how much Paul might have known.[1]

Moral Example

Even though Paul does not provide many explicit details about Jesus's earthly life, the nature of that life as one of servanthood was well known to him, as he reminds his friends in Philippi: "he made himself nothing" (Phil. 2:7). This was as equally a radical departure from Jewish messianic expectations as was a "crucified Messiah." Paul's appeals to his own imitation of Christ, which he in turn expects of his churches as they follow his example (1 Cor. 11:1), are best understood against the backdrop of Paul's knowledge of the life of Jesus. While some of his appeals could refer simply to living a cruciform life—as it surely does in one instance (Phil. 3:15–17) and probably so in another (1 Thess. 1:6–7)—this can hardly be the case in his appeal in 1 Corinthians 11:1, which concludes

---

1. Incidentally, these comments also call into question the current Roman Catholic Church's designation of Jesus's mother as "the Virgin Mary"—at least inasmuch as that designation refers to her perpetual virginity.

his argument with the Corinthians regarding a believer's freedom. In this instance, Paul's *imitatio*, or imitation, refers to his doing everything for the glory of God and thus becoming all things to all people for the sake of the many (1 Cor. 10:31–33). What specific knowledge of Jesus is being assumed here is a matter for speculation, but the very fact that it is assumed is what is so significant. And such speculation could well be grounded in Paul's appeal to "the humility and gentleness of Christ" (2 Cor. 10:1) and to Christ's *splanchnois* ("affections" or "compassion"; Phil. 1:8), which most likely refers to the extraordinary love shown by Christ and also at work in Paul.

That there are not more of these kinds of references in Paul's letters means little since in every case they are quite incidental to some other issue at hand. In each case the historicity of these affirmations is not *argued for* but simply *assumed* and thus *appealed to* as common knowledge among the early followers of Christ. We must constantly remind ourselves that Paul was *not* writing letters with our future interests in view. All of his letters were ad hoc, addressing or encouraging early believers in a variety of historical situations. We are simply privileged to be able to benefit from someone else's mail, as it were, albeit mail that was inspired by the Holy Spirit.

Knowledge of the Teaching of Jesus

For understandable reasons, not much by way of Jesus's actual teaching emerges from Paul's letters. As we said above regarding Jesus's life, Paul's ad hoc concerns were not primarily with what Jesus had to say but with who Jesus was and what he did for humans and our salvation. Nonetheless, as with Paul's references to Jesus's life, so too Paul's references to Jesus's teaching appear at once both offhanded—in the sense that it is obviously assumed to be something held in common between both the Apostle and his readers—and of such diverse nature that once again it suggests that in the preserved Pauline letters we encounter only the tip of the iceberg of Paul's knowledge of Jesus. There are six moments in Paul's writings where he alludes to Jesus's teaching, which we treat here in turn.

1 THESSALONIANS 4:15

According to the Lord's word, we tell you that we who are still alive, who are left until the coming of the Lord, will certainly not precede those who have fallen asleep.

Paul's first reference to Jesus's teaching appears in the earliest letter preserved in the Pauline corpus, 1 Thessalonians, which was written a little less than twenty years after the crucifixion and resurrection of Christ. Here an appeal is made to "the Lord's word" but without quoting it (1 Thess. 4:15). Since Paul uses "the Lord" exclusively to refer to Christ, there can be no question that he is alluding to the teaching of Jesus. Although it could possibly refer to a prophetic word from the risen Lord, more likely it is an appeal to something said by Jesus during his earthly ministry, known by the Apostle and assumed to be available to others and likely actually known to these believers.

GALATIANS 4:6

Because you are his sons, God sent the Spirit of his Son into our hearts, the Spirit who calls out, "*Abba*, Father."

ROMANS 8:15

And by [the Spirit] we cry, "*Abba*, Father."

It is truly remarkable that in the twin passages of Galatians 4:6 and Romans 8:15 Paul asserts that his primarily gentile and therefore Greek-speaking readers are crying out to God as "Father" and are doing so in the language of Jesus himself: *Abba*. Although in the Gospels this language is used by Jesus only in Gethsemane, it is equally a part of his teaching since it undoubtedly lies behind his instructions on how to pray (Matt. 6:9). That this Aramaic word has been maintained even in the Greek-speaking church indicates that here we are dealing with bedrock history regarding the earthly Jesus.[2]

1 CORINTHIANS 7:10

To the married I give this command (not I, but the Lord): A wife must not separate from her husband.

---

2. A similar phenomenon can be found among the forbears of the families Fee (my mother was a Jacobson) and Lofdahl (my wife Maudine's maiden name) with the occasional Swedish *tak sa mycket* ("thank you much").

1 Corinthians 9:14

In the same way, the Lord has commanded that those who preach the gospel should receive their living from the gospel.

1 Corinthians 11:23–25

For I received from the Lord what I also passed on to you: The Lord, Jesus, on the night that he was betrayed, took bread, and when he had given thanks, he broke it and said, "This is my body which is for you; do this in remembrance of me." In the same way, after supper he took the cup, saying, "This cup is the new covenant in my blood; do this, whenever you drink it, in remembrance of me."

In the third letter chronologically in the Pauline corpus, 1 Corinthians, Paul appeals three times to a saying or teaching of Jesus as support for a position that he is espousing. In the first instance (1 Cor. 7:10) he appeals to a saying regarding a wife separating from her husband—a much more unusual form of divorce in the Greco-Roman world than one initiated by the husband. Since Paul's version is adapted to the present situation, it is of little value to pursue the precise nature of its origins, but it clearly reflects what appears in two forms in the Gospels (Mark 10:11 // Matt. 19:9; Luke 16:16 // Matt. 5:32).

In the second appeal to "the Lord" in this letter (1 Cor. 9:14), Paul refers to a command of Jesus as supporting his affirmation that he has the right to material support from the believers in Corinth, even though he has given up that right. This same saying emerges again in a similar context in a much later letter, that "workers deserve their wages" (1 Tim. 5:18), which significantly seems to allude to the language of Luke's Gospel (Luke 10:7), whose author was a gentile believer and friend of Paul.

Finally, in his attempt to correct the abuse of the Lord's table in Corinth, Paul appeals to the words of institution as something he has received from the Lord and has in turn handed on to the Corinthian Christians (1 Cor. 11:23–25). Although there is a degree of ambiguity with regard to what he means by "I received from the Lord," what Paul cites is almost verbatim what appears in Luke's Gospel (Luke 22:17–20; cf. Mark 14:22–25 and Matt. 26:26–29, which reflect a slightly different version). That the form of Paul's saying can be traced specifically to the Gospel tradition of Paul's friend Luke affirms the basic historicity of both the Gospel accounts and the Apostle's knowledge of them.

Again, even though there are only a few references to Jesus's teachings in Paul's writing, those that do appear provide sufficient evidence that there is a much deeper pool of the Jesus tradition from which Paul could cite if he had been so inclined. Why he was less inclined is a matter of speculation, but simple frequency of references is not the important point. That Paul knew about Jesus's life and teachings is incontrovertibly attested in his letters.

Further Knowledge of the Historical Jesus

Along with the places Paul alludes to Jesus's life or teachings, there are several other moments in Paul's letters that indicate Paul's knowledge of the historical Jesus.

PHILIPPIANS 2:6–8

Who, being in very nature God, did not consider equality with God something to be used to his own advantage; rather, he made himself nothing by taking the very nature of a servant, being made in human likeness. And being found in appearance as a man, he humbled himself by becoming obedient to death—even death on a cross!

In a passage that begins with the assertion that Christ existed "in the very nature [or form] of God" but did not tightly grasp his "equality with God" (Phil. 2:6), Paul makes the strongest kinds of statements regarding the genuineness of Jesus's incarnate humanity. This begins with the especially telling metaphor, translated literally as "he poured himself out by taking the form [*morphē*] of a slave." As discussed in chapter 3, the Greek word *morphē* is nearly impossible to render into English since it basically refers to something or someone's outward appearance. But Paul goes on to interpret the metaphor in terms of Christ's "being made in human likeness" (v. 7), which in this context can mean only that, even though Christ had prior existence as God, his incarnation involved being born just as all other humans but without ever losing his divine identity.

The second sentence narrates what Christ did as an *anthrōpos*, or "human," namely, accepting the path to the cross in obedience to his Father (Phil. 2:8). Thus Paul's language simultaneously assumes that at one point in history Christ had not been a human but that when he did become one of us, he was fully and completely so. And only in this way could true redemption have been possible. Christ became one of us so that we might be transformed and thereby conformed to the divine image that had been marred by the fall.

1 Timothy 2:5–6

For there is one God and one mediator between God and mankind, the man Christ Jesus, who gave himself as a ransom for all people.

1 Timothy 3:16

He appeared in the flesh, was vindicated by the Spirit . . . was believed on in the world, was taken up in glory.

In a way similar to what Paul said to the Philippians, 1 Timothy stresses Christ's true humanity when speaking of Christ as the divine mediator between God and humans. The NIV puts it nicely: "For there is . . . one mediator between God and mankind, the man Christ Jesus, who gave himself as a ransom for all people" (1 Tim. 2:5–6)—language that, like Philippians 2, presupposes both choice and obedience. Thus even though the Pauline authorship of 1 Timothy is disputed, its essential theology is thoroughly Pauline. Likewise, the "hymn" in 1 Timothy 3:16 begins with the line, "He appeared in the flesh," once again stressing Christ's true humanity.

Galatians 4:4–5

But when the set time had fully come, God sent his Son, born of a woman, born under the law, to redeem those under the law, that we might receive adoption to sonship. Because you are his sons, God sent the Spirit of his Son into our hearts, the Spirit who calls out, "*Abba*, Father."

Romans 8:3

For what the law was powerless to do because it was weakened by the flesh, God did by sending his own Son in the likeness of sinful flesh to be a sin offering.

Galatians 4:4–5 and Romans 8:3 offer what might be called Paul's "sending formula." In Galatians, the narrative of salvation found in this very brief summary is used at a crucial moment in Paul's argument that Christ's death eliminated the need for Torah observance. Its essential parts put it clearly: "God sent his Son . . . to redeem those under the law." The two middle phrases, which elaborate the first part of the sentence and anticipate the latter, emphasize Christ's humanity: "born of a woman, born under the law." The first phrase eliminates any possibility of a divine Savior who was not truly human; the second places him squarely within a clearly identifiable historical context. So even though Paul is not intending to emphasize Christ's humanity as such, he does so without trying—precisely because this was the common understanding of the early church and thus shared between Paul and his addressees. Indeed, from Paul's perspective this is a *fundamental* reality that makes everything else in the Christian narrative hold together. As we have seen repeatedly, what Paul argues *from*—as a common denominator between himself and his readers—is more significant than arguments *for* what they should believe.

In the second instance of this sending formula, Romans 8:3, the emphasis is especially on Christ's humanity, which enabled him to serve as an adequate sin offering. Thus he came "in the likeness of sinful flesh." Paul's point is that Christ's "flesh," or body, was like all other human bodies; however, unlike the rest of us he did not yield himself to sin. As in Galatians, so too here Paul argues *from* rather than *for* the reality of the incarnation.

GALATIANS 3:16

The promises were spoken to Abraham and to his seed. Scripture does not say "and to seeds," meaning many people, but "and to your seed," meaning one person, who is Christ.

ROMANS 1:3

. . . regarding his Son, who as to his earthly life was a descendant of David.

ROMANS 9:5

From [the people of Israel] is traced the human ancestry of the Messiah, who is God over all, forever praised! Amen.

2 Timothy 2:8
Remember Jesus Christ, raised from the dead, descended from David.

A number of passages present a picture of Jesus's humanity in terms of his status as the long-awaited Jewish Messiah—a picture that will be spelled out in greater detail in part 3. These passages are introduced here because together they demonstrate the presuppositional nature of Paul's understanding of Christ's genuine humanity. Jesus is identified as Abraham's "seed" (Gal. 3:16), the embodiment and culmination of Israel itself; as born of David's lineage (Rom. 1:3; 2 Tim. 2:8); and explicitly as "the Messiah" (Rom. 9:5), the culminating expression of Jewish privileges.

Again, the point in these passages is not about Christ's humanity as such; rather, Christ's humanity is presupposed in the language itself. The same can even be said of Paul's use of *Christos*, or "Christ," as his primary way of identifying the now risen Jesus. Indeed, some have argued that the "name" Jesus Christ always carries with it its titular connotations of Jesus as the Jewish Messiah. Whether or not that is so, this title-turned-name—even when used simply as an identifying referent—harks back to the historical reality that the earthly Jesus lived and died as the Jewish Messiah, whom God raised from the dead to be Lord of all.

Conclusion

In this chapter we have seen that throughout Paul's letters the name "Jesus" always has as its primary referent the historical human, Jesus of Nazareth, whom the Romans crucified and the earliest Christians believed to be the Jewish Messiah and the now risen Lord. While Paul places much of his theological emphasis on the Messiah's redeeming work in his death on the cross, the language of crucifixion never loses its historical bearings. When, for example, Paul speaks of "the Son of God, who loved me and gave himself for me" (Gal. 2:20), he is referring not to the theological outcome of that death but to the historical event of the death itself—the excruciating death by crucifixion at the hands of the (very historical) Roman Empire.

And so it is with every mention of the cross and of Christ's death for us. This event does not begin for Paul as *theology*; it begins as *history*, where a truly human Jesus died as the Jewish Messiah. What Paul came to see clearly is that this historical event, which was humanity's loud "No!" to Jesus of Nazareth, was God's louder "No!" to human sin. The great glory of the biblical narrative is that God has pronounced an exclamatory "Yes!" to everything the Jesus of human history has done for sinners through his death and resurrection to life forever.

Paul concedes that there is one aspect of common humanity that Jesus did not know by experience. While Paul is adamant about the universality of human sinfulness ("all have sinned and fall short of the [intended] glory of God"; Rom. 3:23), he asserts that Christ knew no sin (2 Cor. 5:21), by which he means that Christ had not personally *experienced* sin.[3] Yet even here Paul's very reason for this assertion is to place it in stark contrast with the climactic phrase: "God made him . . . to be sin [or a sin offering] for us" (2 Cor. 5:21). This is the great exchange, and from Paul's perspective it could happen only because the sinless one was nonetheless truly human and came to know our sinfulness not by his own experience of it but by bearing the weight of it in his death on the cross. In all of this, Christ never ceased to be God. This is the mystery that lies at the very heart of the Christian faith, and Paul is one of its primary advocates.

As we will see in parts 3 and 4, Paul's conviction was a combination of two realities: first, that Jesus in his earthly life fulfilled God's promise that David's greater Son would effect final redemption for God's people; and, second, that through his exaltation the eternal Son also assumed the role of the messianic Lord seated at the right hand of the Father—the Lord to whom all are now subject and before whose lordship ultimately "every knee will bow" and "every tongue will acknowledge" (Rom. 14:11, citing Isa. 45:23).

---

3. Indeed, the Hebrew verb "to know" is the primary Jewish way of talking about sexual intercourse (e.g., Gen. 4:1, 25), indicating more than just cognitive knowledge.

PART 3

The Jewish Messiah and Son of God

For Paul, Christ's person and his work are intimately related: it is because of who Christ is that he was able to accomplish what he did, so examining what he accomplished gives us a picture of who he is. Having focused on Paul's understanding of the work of Christ, the redeemer and creator of the new humanity, in parts 1 and 2, we now devote our attention in parts 3 and 4 to Paul's understanding of the person of Christ. Various affirmations in the Apostle's letters indicate that Paul's understanding of Christ's person is twofold: Jesus, the Jewish Messiah, is (1) the preexistent *Son of God* and (2) the exalted *Lord* now seated "at the right hand of God" (Rom. 8:34)—in the ultimate position of authority next to God himself.

Paul's twofold understanding of the person of Christ is based in part on the Jewish Psalter. In Psalm 2:7 God declares that the Messiah is his "son," while in Psalm 110:1 God tells the Messiah, "Sit at my right hand." In part 3, we examine the first part of Paul's understanding of Christ, as the Jewish Messiah and Son of God, by describing how Jesus is anticipated in the story of Israel (chap. 5), fulfills the role of the Davidic Son of God (chap. 6), and is the *eternal* Son of God (chap. 7).

5

The Anticipation of Jesus
in the Story of Israel

P aul's understanding of the person of Christ has its deepest roots
in Jewish messianism, based on the Davidic kingship. Thus an
examination of the Apostle's recognition of Jesus as born of the
"seed of David" will be our starting point, since as Israel's first great
king, David became the singular person in their history who was understood to be God's "son" par excellence. Equally significant is that
David's monarchical descendants were sometimes celebrated as those
who would "forever" sit on his throne. These two matters will be taken
up in chapters 6 and 7. But in the present chapter we must first situate
Paul's understanding of Christ within the broader story of Israel.

In order to examine the christological significance of Jesus as the Son
of God, we can take our lead from Paul's letter to the believers in Rome.
Romans is the least impassioned of the preserved letters, as it was written mostly to people Paul would not have known personally and thus
served as an introduction of the Apostle to those living in the capital of
the Roman Empire. It is also one of the two letters (along with Ephesians)
where the overarching passion of Paul's own apostolic calling—namely,
to see Jew and gentile *together* as one eschatological people of God—is
argued at length. In Romans Paul spells out quite plainly the earthly

origins of Jesus as fundamental to his being the Jewish Messiah. At the climax of Paul's retelling of the biblical story and recounting of all the Jewish privileges, Paul states his anguish over Jewish rejection of their own *Christos*, or Messiah (Rom. 9:5), which scholars agree in this instance is used exclusively as a title for Jesus himself.

So central is this concern on the part of the Apostle that it comes as the first thing in this letter to the believers in Rome, a very large number of whom Paul would not have known personally, despite the long series of greetings at the end (Rom. 16:3–15). Paul begins his careful presentation of his entire understanding of the Christian gospel with a somewhat elaborate salutation in which Jesus is introduced as God's "Son, who as to his earthly life was a descendant of David, and who through the Spirit of holiness was appointed the Son of God in power by his resurrection from the dead: Jesus Christ, our Lord" (1:3–4). It is not surprising, therefore, that in contrast to the rest of Paul's preserved letters, in Romans the *primary* christological motif is of Jesus as the Son of God.

Paul's "Son of God" language is not invented whole cloth but is woven together from language that was already a part of Israel's story. Below we examine how Paul regularly places Christ within that story. We begin where Paul does: with his own encounter with the crucified Jesus as the exalted Lord of a psalm that he and most of his contemporaries considered to be messianic (Ps. 110:1). Indeed, Paul's encounter accounts in large part for his own radically altered understanding of the Messiah as not only exalted but also *crucified*.

The Ultimate Scandal: Jesus as the Crucified Messiah

Norwegian New Testament scholar Nils Dahl observes that scholars sometimes speak of Paul's Christology without ever referring to the messiahship of Jesus, but he then rightly points out that "whether Jesus was the Messiah or not was crucial in the life of the onetime persecutor and later apostle."[1] Dahl's assessment of Paul's view of Christ is confirmed in several passages that are rather early in the Pauline collection.

1. Nils A. Dahl, *Jesus the Christ: The Historical Origins of Christological Doctrine* (Minneapolis: Fortress, 1991), 15.

The historical reality that the religious leaders of Jesus's day tried to eliminate Jesus, at least in part because of a latent claim that he was the Messiah, lies at the heart of Paul's understanding. What was intolerable for them was a Messiah who lived and taught in ways that ran roughshod over their own understanding and expectations. They were looking for more normal signs of power, power that would free them from the bondage of belonging to a pagan foreign power. What they got instead was power of a radically different kind, packaged in the form of gentleness and meekness—but still very real power indeed! From any merely human perspective it is no wonder these leaders wanted to do away with him: he was so totally off most people's radar or expectations for who the Messiah would be!

To be sure, in the sometimes unfortunate history of the later church, there has been a deluge of attempts to re-create Christ back into our own fallen images. Why, we seem to wonder rather constantly, can't God be just a bit more like us so that we can ultimately fall down and worship one who has been re-created in our own image? But that will not work now any more than it did then, because at the very heart of our story lies that ultimate theological oxymoron: a crucified Messiah! And so it was for Paul, in ever so many ways. So we begin where Paul began, with what he called from a merely human perspective, "the foolishness of God."

1 CORINTHIANS 1:22–25
Jews demand signs and Greeks look for wisdom, but we preach Christ crucified: a stumbling block to Jews and foolishness to Gentiles, but to those whom God has called, both Jews and Greeks, Christ the power of God and the wisdom of God. For *the foolishness of God* is wiser than human wisdom, and the weakness of God is stronger than human strength.

1 CORINTHIANS 15:3
Christ died for our sins according to the Scriptures.

Toward the end of his first letter to the Corinthians, Paul takes up the issue of the future bodily resurrection of believers, an idea that was especially repulsive to these believers, who were apparently looking for something a bit more "spiritual." At the outset Paul reminds them of what has been "passed on" to them, that the One who was raised bodily from the dead is the same "Christ" who had "died for our sins" (1 Cor. 15:3). In so doing, Paul appears to be citing the basic elements of an early creedal formula that was held in common by the earliest community of believers. But, interestingly, this formula comes at the very *end* of the letter, where Paul finally confronts those who were denying a future bodily resurrection of believers. Therefore, and even if not by Paul's design, this passage serves as an *inclusio* with—and must be understood in light of—the *first* item addressed in the letter (1:13–2:5). At the outset, with considerable irony and passion, Paul reminds these believers of "the foolishness of God" (1:25), reflected first in the message of a "Christ crucified" (1:18–25); then in the Corinthian believers themselves, of whom not many were "wise by human standards," "influential," or "of noble birth" (1:26–31); and finally in God's calling Paul, who came not "with eloquence or human wisdom," to be an *apostle* (2:1–5). It is therefore little wonder that there was some considerable tension between Paul and the Corinthians: Greek wisdom was much more to their liking than any emphasis on Christ as the crucified one, the ultimate shame for any Roman citizen in such an important city as Corinth.

Paul's argument makes sense contextually only if, when he writes "Christ crucified" (1 Cor. 1:23), he means a crucified *Messiah*. This in particular was the ultimate "stumbling block," or scandal, for the Jews. At the same time it would have been such utter folly to the Greeks that one can only wonder why Paul would so vehemently press *this* point with the Corinthians as the first thing in his letter. Why not simply let Christ be a proper name and put the emphasis on his death "for us"? But no, Paul says, we preach a *crucified* Messiah, knowing full well how both Jews and Greeks will respond: "scandal" to the one and "foolishness" to the other (v. 23). Why does Paul do this? Because, he maintains, in God's own infinite wisdom and power, every imaginable human pretension—that we should consider ourselves as able either to find out God or to match wits with God—has been undercut.

One will simply never understand Paul, nor the depth of his commitment and devotion to Christ, without starting where he starts: with the crucified Messiah. This is why Dahl's observation noted above rings so true, and it leads us to seek for Paul's own reasons for such a proclamation, especially when he knew full well how people on both sides of the ethnic "wall of separation" would instinctively resist it as either "scandal" or "foolishness." Answering this question leads us back to the Apostle's own story, which finds expression on several occasions, but especially so at two crucial moments in his letters: first, in an impassioned defense of his own apostleship to the Galatians and, second, in a letter to the Philippians that has all the markings of a letter of friendship with one of his truly beloved communities of faith.

GALATIANS 1:15–16

But when God, who set me apart from my mother's womb and called me by his grace, was pleased to reveal his Son in me so that I might preach him among the Gentiles, my immediate response was not to consult any human being.

PHILIPPIANS 3:4–6

If someone else thinks they have reasons to put confidence in the flesh, I have more: circumcised on the eighth day, of the people of Israel, of the tribe of Benjamin, a Hebrew of Hebrews; in regard to the law, a Pharisee; as for zeal, persecuting the church; as for righteousness based on the law, faultless.

Early on in the argument of Paul's letter to the believers in Galatia, while demonstrating that his version of the gospel was without human origins of any kind—and was therefore not dependent on those in Jerusalem who were apostles before him—Paul points to the radical nature of his own conversion. He begins by asserting that he had advanced far beyond others in Judaism in two ways: (1) as a persecutor of the perceived enemy, the Christ-followers, and (2) as an avid student of Torah (Gal. 1:13–14). Although the second of these is perhaps more important in the long run, he mentions being a persecutor of the church first in this instance very likely because this is what had most clearly distanced him from the early believing community. For the Apostle, his zeal in persecuting Christ-followers both demonstrated his independence from his readers and put him on the other side of any of those who had followed Jesus as the Jewish Messiah. Indeed, there was absolutely nothing in Paul's personal history that would ever have led him to become a follower of Christ, and yet he had become one—and passionately so!

Incidentally, the later narrative by Luke in Acts 9:1–2 agrees with Paul's self-assessment at this point.

The sentence that follows this preconversion autobiographical moment begins in an especially significant way: "But when God, who . . . called me by his grace, was pleased to reveal his Son *in me* so that I might preach him among the Gentiles, my immediate response was not to consult any human being" (Gal. 1:15–16). The prepositional phrase Paul uses here, noted in italics above, has had an unfortunate history in the English versions, having occasionally been rendered as *to me* (e.g., NRSV, ESV). But this is a case where translators make Paul say what they want him to have said, since it plays havoc with a Greek preposition that simply cannot in any way be stretched to carry that meaning.

To the contrary, in telling his own story at this early moment in the letter, the Apostle puts forth the thoroughly radical nature of his own conversion from a Christ hater to a Christ devotee. He deliberately sets himself forward as Exhibit A of the gospel of grace that includes both Jew and gentile. God chose to reveal his Son *in* Saul of Tarsus, meaning that Paul served personally as a thoroughly unlikely candidate to exhibit God's redeeming love and grace.

To be sure, this moment has appeared to many as little more than a passing moment in his letter to the Galatian believers. But that it was not just an incidental moment, struck on the hot iron of controversy, is confirmed by Paul's stress on the same two points in his much later retelling of his story. In writing to the believers in Philippi, in what is known technically as a "letter of friendship," Paul again sets forth his unquestioned Jewish credentials (Phil. 3:4–6). In this case he does so, first, in terms of what had been given to him at birth (circumcised, of the tribe of Benjamin, an Israelite of Israelites) and, second, in terms of his own achievements within Judaism (a zealous Pharisee who had both persecuted the church and been a faultless adherent of the law). The order in which the two realities are affirmed would seem to reflect his own self-understanding of the significance of his former posture toward Christ and his followers. He had tried to eliminate the early communities of believers precisely because they were worshiping one whom he could only believe that God had rejected by having him crucified by the Roman Empire.

In both of these retellings of what is essential to his pre-Christian story, Paul places his violence against the church before his loyal adherence to the law. Most likely this is the result of his own controversies within the Jewish community, where he was wont to remind fellow Jews that he had once been where they are. So again he juxtaposes his past as both a persecutor of the church and a faithful adherent of the law with the surpassing worth of knowing Christ as Lord, putting all of these former privileges into the category of *zēmia* (Phil. 3:7), a Greek word that has to do with something basically worthless, something to be thrown away, which the KJV translators properly rendered as "dung."

Thus the common denominator of Paul's pre-Christian life was that he was an avid follower of Torah and an equally avid persecutor of those who dared proclaim that the crucified Jesus was the Jewish Messiah, which was the ultimate scandal for a law-abiding man like Saul of Tarsus. The God he served with passion could not possibly have been involved in such foolishness, which is why Paul considered his own encounter with the risen Christ to be of the same kind as all those that had preceded him, even though it was untimely.

GALATIANS 3:13

Christ redeemed us from the curse of the law by becoming a curse for us, for it is written: "Cursed is everyone who is hung on a pole" [Deut. 21:23].

We learn the reason for Saul of Tarsus's hatred for followers of Jesus in Paul's letter to the believers in Galatia, where the Apostle associates Christ's death by crucifixion with the curse of Deuteronomy: "Cursed [by God] is anyone who is hung on a pole" (Gal. 3:13). Since Jesus had been "hung on a pole" by the Romans, this had served for Saul as sure evidence that the one and only God had "cursed" Jesus, and he whom God had cursed could not possibly be honored as the Jewish Messiah. This in particular accounts for Saul's considerable passion to eliminate what he perceived as an absolute heresy. The God of Israel could not possibly have done something so utterly foolish—so absolutely contrary to what would have happened had God consulted us for wisdom!

Thus it was no mere bit of cleverness, but words spoken out of personal experience, that had led Paul earlier to argue with the Corinthians (1 Cor.

1:21–24, discussed above) that what from any merely human perspective is the ultimate oxymoron—a crucified Messiah—must be recognized as *God's* power and wisdom at work in the world. As we discussed above, the historical event that was viewed as sheer folly by those who spoke Greek (namely, the gentile world) was at the same time an utter scandal to the everyday Jew—and all the more so to a passionately religious one like Saul of Tarsus.

That this scandal lies at the heart of Paul's pre-Christian understanding of Jesus of Nazareth helps to explain the self-description of Paul in a much later letter as formerly "a blasphemer and a persecutor and a violent man" (1 Tim. 1:13). Such a prior commitment to violent opposition explains the radical nature of Saul's conversion in the Damascus road experience, which he relates in terms of *seeing* the Lord (1 Cor. 9:1). Here is an undoubted case where the *effect* (Paul's utter and total devotion to Christ as Lord) must be commensurate with the *cause* (being confronted by the crucified one as the risen one). His personal encounter with the risen Jesus radicalized Paul (cf. 1 Cor. 15:8). It also explains his immediate departure to Arabia (Gal. 1:17), very likely as a compulsion to go to historic Mount Sinai, the place where God had given the law to Moses, to sort out what had happened to him on the road to Damascus.

Thus Paul emerged from his Damascus road experience as a passionate follower of God's true Messiah, Jesus, crucified and raised from the dead. What Paul eventually came to realize, as the argument in his letter to the Galatians indicates (Gal. 3:10–14), is that the hanging of Christ on a cross did indeed involve God's curse, just not on Christ as such. Rather, the whole human race in their sin and rebellion against the eternal God came under God's curse, and in effect humanity was hung on the cross through the one perfect sacrifice so that all could be raised to eternal life. True wisdom indeed!

God's paradoxical wisdom lies at the very heart of the Christ narrative: that the eternal One should so love his created ones that he would go to such lengths to redeem them and by his Spirit to re-create them in the divine image. This is why any theology of redemption that does not include behavior as the necessary result of the essential Christian story falls far short of the Apostle himself. In Paul's view, to be sure, we are not saved *by* good works, but we are indeed saved *for* good works, in the sense of doing what is good for one and all. Any theology that falls short of this does not in any way reflect Paul's own passions.

For Paul, humankind's "No" to Christ was in fact God's "No" to our fallenness and rebellion, whereby we were offered grace and eternal glory. And by raising Christ from the dead, God said "Yes" to the Son and thus to humankind through the Son. The result, Paul argues, was that what was for any good Jew the ultimate oxymoron—a crucified Messiah—turns out to be the ultimate expression of God's own *wisdom and power* over against every form of human machination. Only the eternal God in his infinite wisdom could be so wise as to be so "foolish" from our merely human perspective.

The theme of a crucified Messiah is a sure instance where the often cited scholarly criterion of "frequency of mention" is quite unrelated to theological significance. That Paul does not refer more often either to his own conversion or to Christ as a crucified Messiah has little or no bearing at all on the importance of this event for Paul's subsequent theological understanding. Rather, what emerges with a kind of frequency that is theologically compelling is the sheer volume of Paul's references to the risen Lord, Jesus, as (the) "Christ."

Even if one grants that by the time of Paul's letters the title "Christ" had moved very close to a name in its own right, the messianic origins of this "name" could hardly have been fully abandoned by this point. In Paul's case this is evidenced by the considerable frequency of every imaginable combination of names and titles in the corpus, including the Pastoral letters, except the combination "the Lord Christ," which appears only twice (Rom. 16:18; Col. 3:24). That the combination occurs at all indicates that the title had become something of a name; yet its infrequency in comparison with all the other combinations would lead one to think that Paul had himself come to this slowly. Thus in time the truly human Jesus, the crucified Messiah, came to be understood as the *Lord*.

Since "Christ," this title-turned-name, derives directly out of Paul's understanding of Jesus as the Jewish Messiah, we can trace this understanding by way of Paul's relationship to the basic narrative of his deeply held commitment to historic Judaism. Whatever else is true of Paul's Christology, he was convinced that the crucified and now risen Christ is the culmination of the basic Jewish story, as a passage in his letter to the believers in Rome bears eloquent testimony.

ROMANS 9:1–5

I speak the truth in Christ—I am not lying, my conscience confirms it through the Holy Spirit—I have great sorrow and unceasing anguish in my heart. For I could wish that I myself were cursed and cut off from Christ for the sake of my people, those of my own race, the people of Israel. Theirs is the adoption to sonship; theirs the divine glory, the covenants, the receiving of the law, the temple worship and the promises. Theirs are the patriarchs, and from them is traced the human ancestry of the Messiah, *who is God* over all, forever praised. Amen.

Paul's cry over his people in Romans 9 is not the rant of a madman but the expression of the deep conviction of one whom Christ had "arrested" on the road to Damascus. And Paul, who seems to have been a passionate individual by nature, redirects all his passion to the One who had now become his "Lord"—namely, the historic Jesus of Nazareth, whom Paul was convinced was none other than the Jewish Messiah. Nothing else can explain how this passionate Christ hater had become such an equally passionate Christ lover. Indeed, so convinced is Paul of Christ's lordship that this passage provides the one certain place where Paul's otherwise consistent usage breaks down and he uses the name "God" specifically to refer to the "Messiah," or Christ (v. 5). While Paul's new understanding of the Jewish Messiah is indeed radical, he returns to Scripture to help him make sense of it. And in so doing he interprets Christ with the basic narrative of Judaism.

Christ and the Basic Narrative of Judaism

Paul cites or echoes the Old Testament in over two hundred instances and in a variety of ways throughout the thirteen letters.[2] Since the Apostle

2. Note that throughout his letters Paul relied on a Greek translation of the Hebrew Bible that came eventually to be known as the Septuagint (LXX), the Bible that was used in all of the Greek-speaking Jewish communities. This was the Bible he would have grown up with in Tarsus and the Bible used by his Greek-speaking churches. This explains why Paul's citations of the Old Testament often differ (at times considerably so) from many English versions since

tended to cite the Old Testament primarily in argumentation, the majority of these references are understandably in Paul's more argumentative letters: the two letters to the believers in Corinth, the one to the believers in Rome, and the one to believers in the province of Galatia. But the letters that are often regarded as having no citations (e.g., 1 and 2 Thessalonians, Colossians, Philippians) are full of equally important echoes of the Old Testament in such crucial ways and with such frequency that one must assume that Paul expected his readers, or hearers, for the most part to have been able to pick up these echoes.[3]

When one turns to look at Paul's use of the Old Testament in general, what stands out is that his primary interest lies with the central features of Israel's essential story:

1. creation
2. Abraham (with the promise of gentile inclusion)
3. the exodus (including both deliverance from bondage and gaining the inherited land)
4. the giving of the law (especially Deuteronomy, with its anticipation of Israel's failure regarding the law)
5. the Davidic kingship
6. the exile and promised restoration (often understood as eschatological consummation), which especially included gentiles

It is not surprising, therefore, that even though Paul cites passages from all over the Greek Old Testament, the considerable majority (over 70 percent) of his citations come from Genesis, Deuteronomy, Isaiah, and the Psalter.

---

our versions have all been translated directly from the Hebrew Bible. This means that in modern English Bibles Paul's "citations" are *two* languages removed from the original: they are an English translation of the Greek translation of the Hebrew Bible! Thus the *content* is usually the same, but the *way* it is said is understandably sometimes a bit different.

3. To be sure, some contemporary readers might be skeptical that Paul's original recipients would have heard these echoes. Since our overloaded culture has multiplied forms of verbal experiences, the idea that people might remember any of them by rote seems altogether unlikely. But this author knows from experience—as any parent who reads to their children will—that even today children are capable of rote memorization. Indeed, once when reading from a familiar children's book to our four children, I slightly changed the story for the fun of it and was immediately reprimanded, "Daddy, that's not how that story goes!"

What is most striking is the role that Christ plays in the story, as the story itself has now been adjusted to *incorporate* Christ as crucified, raised, and exalted. Indeed, for the Apostle his Lord, Jesus Christ, now plays a major role in all six of the primary facets of the story. Chapter 6 focuses on the fifth and sixth items: the Davidic kingship and the eschatological consummation. But first we conclude this chapter with a brief overview of the role Christ plays in the first four elements of the story, which at the same time serves to heighten the effect of the whole picture—that Christ, who is first of all the *messianic* Son of God, is at the same time the *eternal* Son of God.

Creation

1 CORINTHIANS 8:6

Yet for us there is but one God, the Father, from whom all things came and for whom we live; and there is but one Lord, Jesus Christ, through whom all things came and through whom we live.

COLOSSIANS 1:15–16

The Son is the image of the invisible God, the firstborn over all creation. For in him all things were created: things in heaven and on earth, visible and invisible, whether thrones or powers or rulers or authorities; all things have been created through him and for him.

The role of Christ in creation is writ large in two major christological texts in the corpus: 1 Corinthians 8:6 and Colossians 1:15–16. In one of the strange bypaths of New Testament scholarship, some have tried to see Paul in these two moments as echoing personified Wisdom's alleged role in creation. But as we saw in chapter 2, careful examination of these two otherwise unrelated moments in Paul's letters reveals that Paul is not equating Christ with Lady Wisdom. Rather, in each case what is either implied (1 Corinthians) or explicit (Colossians) is that Jesus *as the Son of God* is the divine agent of creation. By identifying God as Father in the Corinthians passage and specifically identifying Christ as the Father's beloved Son in Colossians, Paul places creation firmly in the context of Jesus as the messianic and eternal Son of God.

Paul's use of prepositions in the striking moment in his letter to the Corinthians is revealing: "from" and "for" the Father; "through" and "through" the Son, who in this case is identified as "one Lord, Jesus Christ." Similarly, in writing later to the Colossian believers Paul urges that *everything* that exists came through the agency of the beloved (eternal) Son, who is expressly identified as the sphere (*in him*), the agent (*though him*), and goal (*for him*) of the whole created order. It is difficult to imagine a stronger affirmation of Christ's identity as the eternal Son than this one—even though doing so was not Paul's goal. So, once again, the thoroughly presuppositional nature of what Paul says and his readers understood here reveals a Christology of the highest order.

Abraham

GALATIANS 3:16, 29

The promises were spoken to Abraham and to his seed. Scripture does not say "and to seeds," meaning many people, but "and to your seed," meaning one Person, who is Christ. . . . If you belong to Christ, then you are Abraham's seed, and heirs according to the promise.

ROMANS 8:32

He did not spare his own Son, but gave him up for us all—how will he not also, along with him, graciously give us all things?

Basic to the way the Jewish Bible presented God's dealings with his people was the role of Abraham as progenitor of God's elect people. This fundamental affirmation plays a major role on two occasions where Paul refers to the story: Galatians 3 and Romans 8. As in creation, Christ plays the crucial role in the (now eschatological) retelling of the story of redemption. Thus in Paul's rather strong letter to the believers in Galatia, Christ is identified as the true "seed" of Abraham (Gal. 3:16) so that all who "belong to Christ" are to be understood now as having become Abraham's true "heirs" (v. 29).

In the argument of Paul's later letter to the believers in Rome, the role of Christ with regard to Abraham is spelled out in a slightly different way that in the end comes to the same conclusion. Abraham again is the ancestor of all people who believe, Jews and gentiles alike. But in this case, Abraham offers the key to much of the story: (1) he is the exemplary man of faith in that (2) he trusted God *before* circumcision and is thus the father of gentiles who believe (Rom. 4:9–11); at the same time (3) he received circumcision as an expression of his faith and is thus also the father of the Jews, now especially of those who have similar faith (v. 12); and (4) he serves as the primary example of faith through the birth of Isaac, whom he received as one raised from the dead, which in turn leads to our faith in the One who was truly raised from the dead (vv. 18–25).

Echoing the narrative of Isaac—specifically Genesis 22:16—later in his letter (Rom. 8:32), Paul has Christ step into the role of the promised Son. Just as God blessed Abraham because he did not spare his beloved son, so now God is portrayed as stepping into Abraham's role as the one who *"did not spare his own Son."* What is striking in this kind of echo of an Old Testament passage is the ease with which Paul does this; most likely he assumes that at least some of his readers will hear the echo and thereby see the relationship of the two narratives.

Thus each mention in Paul's letters of Abraham and his role in the basic biblical story is explicitly tied to Christ. With Christ's coming, the promise to Abraham that all nations would be blessed has found its fulfillment.

The Exodus

COLOSSIANS 1:12–16

... giving joyful thanks to *the Father,* who has qualified *you* to *share in the inheritance* of *his holy people* [traditionally "saints"] in the kingdom of light. For he has *rescued us* from the *dominion of darkness* and brought us into *the kingdom of the Son he loves,* in whom we have *redemption,* the forgiveness of sins. The Son is the *image* of the invisible God, the *firstborn* over all creation. For *in him all things were created*: things in heaven and on earth, visible and invisible, whether thrones or powers or rulers or authorities; *all things have been created through him and for him.*

The exodus as part of the biblical story comes through in many ways in Paul's letters, primarily in the passages dealing with salvation, which are too many to note here individually. Indeed, every metaphor for salvation in Christ except "reconciliation," which is also the least metaphorical term, comes directly from the Pentateuch, especially the theme of "redemption." One passage in particular, Colossians 1:12–16, echoes much of the story of the exodus, including gaining the inherited land, while at the same time alluding to the other major moments in Israel's story, which we have italicized above. Below we lay out the many allusions in this passage:

1. Creation: He is *before* all things, which were all created *in him* and *through him* and exist *for* him.
2. Abraham: The language of "Son he loves" (cf. Gen. 22:2, 16) begins here.
3. Exodus: (a) The verb "rescued" and noun "redemption" both echo Exodus 6:6, a crucial moment in the story of Israel; (b) the deliverance is from the "dominion of darkness."
4. The law: While not treated explicitly in this passage, it emerges as the central issue a bit later (2:6–23).
5. Kingship: (a) the Son brings us into "the kingdom"; (b) the Son is God's beloved; (c) the Son is God's "firstborn" (*prōtotokos*, as in Exod. 4:22 and Ps. 89:26–27).
6. The eschatological inclusion of the gentiles: This is signaled by the interchange of "you" and "us."

And all of these themes are found in just one, very long, typically Pauline sentence! In Paul's letters, Christ is regularly seen as the way the new covenant fulfillment of the story takes place, and thus he is understood as *in continuity* with the first expression of the story. Indeed, in a series of warnings to the Corinthian believers, drawn from Israel's own history, Paul expressly understood Christ to have been present with Israel in that first expression of the story: "they drank from the spiritual rock that accompanied them, and that rock was Christ," and "we should not test Christ, as some of them did" (1 Cor. 10:4, 9).

The Giving of the Law

ROMANS 10:4

Christ is the culmination [= goal] of the law so that there may be righteousness for everyone who believes.

The giving of the law is perhaps the most widely recognized element of Israel's history that Paul argues has been fulfilled with the coming of Christ. Nonetheless, this emphasis occurs in Paul in only four instances, all of which have in common the threat of gentile believers' capitulating to Torah observance (Romans; Galatians; Philippians 3; Colossians 2). In Romans 10:4, Paul makes this connection so directly that it requires no further commentary.

Conclusion

We conclude our abbreviated review of Paul's use of Israel's narrative by emphasizing once again the primary concern—to note that Paul simply asserts that Christ was both *present* at key places in the original unfolding of the biblical story and is *the central feature* of its current unfolding in human history. As we'll see in chapter 6, Christ plays the major role in the crucial fifth and sixth elements of the story, which serve as the key matters in Paul's Christology. We thus turn to an examination of the related themes of Jesus as (1) the Jewish Messiah who at the same time is (2) the eternal Son of God.

6

Jesus as the Son of David

I n order to appreciate how Paul came to understand Jesus as the eternal Son of God in terms of the Davidic kingship, we must briefly examine several key moments from the biblical story itself—including the role of the historical Jesus in the story. The concern here is to point out the presuppositions Paul would have brought to his understanding of Jesus as the long-awaited Jewish Messiah, and we do so because this is the background that is regularly assumed by the Apostle as common ground between himself and his (now mostly gentile) readers.

Jesus as the Davidic Son of God

In the story of the exodus, Yahweh instructs Moses to tell the ruler of Egypt, "This is what the LORD [= Yahweh] says: Israel is my firstborn son, and I told you, 'Let my son go, so he may worship me.' But you refused to let him go; so I will kill your firstborn son" (Exod. 4:22–23). Here Yahweh uses a play on words to describe what would happen to the Egyptians: *Israel* as a people are designated both as God's "son" and God's "firstborn," thus anticipating the death of all of Egypt's firstborn males. This theme is picked up much later by the prophet Hosea, who quotes Yahweh: "When Israel was a child, I loved him, and out of Egypt I called my son" (Hosea 11:1).

In time, this designation of "son" was applied to Israel's king, who was understood both as God's representative to Israel and especially as standing in for the people before God. As the story progresses the king is regularly designated as God's son, including at a crucial turning point in the story: the Davidic covenant, where Yahweh declares to King David, "I will raise up your offspring to succeed you, your own flesh and blood, . . . and I will establish the throne of his kingdom forever. I will be his father, and he will be my son" (2 Sam. 7:12–14).

In response to this promise we are told that "King David went in and sat before the LORD and said: 'Who am I, Sovereign LORD, and what is my family, that you have loved me in this way?'" (2 Sam. 7:18 LXX). Thus in the Davidic covenant, David's progeny are called "God's sons," while David himself responds that lying behind this promise is God's love for him.

The theme of the king as God's "son" is especially prominent in the Psalter, serving to frame the so-called Davidic Psalter (books 1 and 2; Pss. 1–41 and 42–72), which signs off with a note from the collector: "This concludes the prayers of David son of Jesse" (Ps. 72:20). Significantly, this is the first instance in the Old Testament where the "kingly son" is also called the Lord's "anointed," which in the Septuagint is translated *ho Christos*, meaning Yahweh's "anointed one."

In Psalm 2, which introduces Israel's king as the one who stands in for the people with laments and praises to God, the psalmist declares that the king is both "God's *Christos*" and "God's *son*," and that the nations (= gentiles) will become his inheritance: "The kings of the earth rise up and the rulers band together against the LORD and against his *anointed* [Gk. *Christos*]" (2:2). "He said to me: 'You are my *son*; today I have become your father. Ask me, and I will make the nations your inheritance, the ends of the earth your possession'" (2:7–8).

Similarly, and with apparent thoughtfulness, the collector of the Psalter used a psalm of Solomon as the bookend of the first two books. The theme of sonship appears again in the opening words of Psalm 72, and thus as the framing device for the initial Davidic Psalter: "Endow the king with your justice, O God, the royal son with your righteousness" (72:1).

Finally, it was the "eternal" nature of the Davidic covenant that elicited Ethan the Ezrahite's plaintive cry in Psalm 89:26–27 (88:27–28 in the LXX). This psalm was composed during the exile in light of the apparent demise of both the king and Jerusalem. As the psalmist recites the promises of God's covenant with David (vv. 20–38), he reminds God of the eternal One's own declaration, which begins: "I have found David my servant; with my sacred oil I have anointed him. My hand will sustain him; surely my arm will strengthen him" (vv. 20–21). In so doing Ethan was reflecting the reality that the king stood in for the people, the original "firstborn son" (Exod. 4:22–23), who as "son" is also God's "anointed one" (*Christos*).

As this abbreviated review indicates, as Paul studied the Scriptures his Lord both was present at key moments in the first unfolding of the story and is the central feature of its current eschatological unfolding. It is therefore no surprise that Christ plays the major role in the crucial fifth and sixth elements of the story, which serve as the foundation for Paul's Christology.

The Story of Jesus in the Gospels

Israel's narrative eventually brings us to Jesus himself, who, according to the Synoptic tradition (Matthew, Mark, Luke), presented himself to Israel as its long-expected messianic king and thus took unto himself all the Davidic titles except "firstborn." Indeed, the primary themes are already put in place at his baptism with the voice from heaven—"You are my Son, whom I love" (Luke 3:22; cf. Ps. 2:7)—and is reinforced by Jesus's use of two passages from Deuteronomy to respond to the tempter in the wilderness: "Man shall not live on bread alone" (Luke 4:4; cf. Deut. 8:3) and "Worship the Lord your God and serve Him only" (Luke 4:8; cf. Deut. 6:13). In these back-to-back stories from the beginning of Jesus's ministry, Jesus steps into the role of Israel as God's Son, passing through the waters and spending forty days in the wilderness—but succeeding precisely at the points where Israel failed when they were tested forty years in the wilderness. And these stories are followed immediately in the Gospel narratives with Jesus going forth to pronounce the advent of the kingdom of God (see Luke 4:14–21).

Jesus's baptism and temptation took place with few to no outside observers. So how do the Gospel writers know about these events where Jesus steps into the role of Israel as God's son and by implication into the messianic role of Israel's *king* as God's son? There are two possible answers: (1) that this is the creation of the later church, which had come to believe this about him, or (2) that Jesus himself had disclosed it to the inner circle. While we affirm the latter alternative, the relevant point here is simply that this narrative is quite in keeping with what Paul had come to believe about Christ some years before the Gospels had been written. And since Paul, by his own testimony, had little association with the early Aramaic-speaking followers of Jesus, he can hardly be accused of creating this view of the historical Jesus.

Likewise, the series of conflict stories between Jesus and the Jewish leaders, as they appear in the Synoptic Gospels, presents the picture that emerges in Paul's writing. This comes out especially in the way these narratives were arranged in Mark's Gospel (12:1–37 // Matt. 21:33–22:46 // Luke 21:9–47), where one can scarcely miss the nature of the disclosure. The center section of this series of five pericopes offers three kinds of conflicts between Jesus and the Jewish leaders: on paying the imperial tax to Caesar (Mark 12:13–17); on the question of the resurrection of the dead (vv. 18–27); and on the question of the greatest commandment (vv. 28–34). These conflicts are framed by two stories in which Jesus takes the initiative. The first, the parable of the tenants in the vineyard, openly asserts a *Son of God* Christology, where God's final envoy to Israel is his beloved Son. This parable also embeds a reference to a messianic Psalm regarding "the stone the builders rejected" (Mark 12:10–11; cf. Ps. 118:22–23). Equally significant is the way the series of five pericopes concludes with an *exalted Lord* Christology, where Jesus's point is that he is more than merely a son of David. According to Jesus, the Son of God is none other than the exalted Lord who is to assume the high honor of sitting at Yahweh's right hand, as affirmed at the beginning of what both postexilic Jews and early Christians understood to be a messianic Psalm: "The Lord said to my Lord: 'Sit at my right hand until I put your enemies under your feet'" (Mark 12:36; cf. Ps. 110:1).

Thus, according to the Gospel accounts, Son of God Christology finds its beginnings in Israel's narrative. And as with the early Synoptic Gospels and later Gospel of John, so it is also with Paul. Son of God Christology therefore simply cannot be, as some have mistakenly argued, the creation of the later church as the story gets reinterpreted in light of Greek modes of thought. That the Messiah is God's Son is a biblical notion at its very core. What surprises everyone is that the messianic king of Israel, God's true Son, is not simply one more in the line of David but turns out to be the *incarnate* Son, who in his incarnation reveals true sonship and true kingship. This in turn is also what makes the crucifixion both a radical moment of Roman injustice and the ultimate outpouring of divine love for one and all.

Jesus as the Eschatological King and Son of God

While Paul's writings present the theme of Davidic sonship less overtly than the Gospels, arguably such an understanding of the Jewish Messiah—and of Jesus as that Messiah—lies behind the telling moments when Paul does momentarily lift the veil. Indeed, at the outset of Romans, the letter whose ultimate concern is Jew and gentile *together* as the one eschatological people of God, Paul offers an elaborate introduction that includes the words "promised," "Son," and "David" (Rom. 1:2–3).

Later in the letter, at the beginning of a long narration of God's faithfulness to Israel, Paul's litany of anguish reads:

> I could wish that I myself were cursed and cut off from Christ for the sake of my people, those of my own race, the people of Israel. Theirs is the adoption to sonship; theirs is the divine glory, the covenants, the receiving of the law, the temple worship and the promises. Theirs are the patriarchs, and from them is traced the human ancestry of the Messiah [Gk. *Christos*], who is God over all, forever praised! Amen. (Rom. 9:3–5)

Here Paul specifically identifies Jesus as the Jewish Messiah, as the NIV translators have rightly rendered it. To be sure, this is the same word that elsewhere is consistently rendered "Christ," but such a translation at this point would miss what Paul is asserting. This is the one sure place in his letters where the Apostle's use of *Christos* clearly functions as a title, not a name. Paul thus reinforces the picture presented in the Gospels that Jesus is the Christ, or Messiah, of Israel.

At some early point in Paul's letters, this *title* became the Savior's primary *name*, "Christ." Indeed, in his extant letters the Apostle uses this name considerably more often than what had now become the primary *title*, "the Lord." A similar transition can be seen in Paul's use of "Son of God" language. This language is rooted in Jewish messianism, but because of the Apostle's conviction of the Son's *preexistence*, it is also used to refer to the pre-incarnate divine Son. For Paul, Son of God Christology does not *begin* in eternity; it begins with the Old Testament narrative of God's dealings with Israel. Nonetheless, this language has meaning for him far beyond its historical messianic origins. This shift in perspective can be seen most clearly in three places in Paul's letters where the relationship between Christ as the kingly, and thus messianic, Son of God merges with the greater reality that the kingly (messianic) Son is in fact the eternal Son of God—sent into the world in order to re-create us as God's true children.

ROMANS 1:1–4

Paul, a servant of Christ Jesus, called to be an apostle and set apart for the gospel of God—the gospel he promised beforehand through his prophets in the Holy Scriptures regarding his Son, who as to his earthly life was a descendant of David, and who through the Spirit of holiness was appointed Son of God in power by his resurrection from the dead: Jesus Christ our Lord.

In the prologue of Romans, the Apostle states that the gospel he preaches was promised *beforehand* through the prophets and that the now-fulfilled promise is about God's Son, who in his earthly life was a descendant of David. But he is now to be known as the "Son of God in power" (Rom. 1:4), predicated on his having been raised from the dead. Although probably not intended as such, here is the one certain place in Paul's letters where Davidic Son and eternal Son merge. Based on this passage alone, one might be tempted to settle for an adoptionist Christology, where Jesus becomes the "eternal" Son at his resurrection and subsequent exaltation. But the rest of the letter forbids such a view. The last phrases in this remarkable preamble to the letter should be understood as the vindication by both the Father and the Spirit of the eternal Son, who had previously been sent by the Father "in the likeness of sinful flesh" (8:3) so as to be the divine sin offering—which is the starting point of our becoming children of God as well.

Early on in the narrative of his own calling with which he begins his letter to the Galatians, Paul states that God was pleased to reveal his Son *in* Paul himself (Gal. 1:16). Paul is not thinking of the Son's origins as the heir to the Davidic throne but is expressing eternal realities. God's Son is not simply the messianic king, sent by the Father to deliver Israel from bondage; he is the one whom the Father sent to earth to redeem God's people and give them adoption as "sons" so that they too may become full heirs—not now of a strip of land on the eastern Mediterranean shore but of eternity itself. Indeed, as Paul urges in Romans 8, the redeemed are joint heirs with the "firstborn" into whose image they are being re-created (vv. 17 and 29).

1 CORINTHIANS 15:23–27

But each in turn: Christ, the firstfruits; then, when he comes, those who belong to him. Then the end will come, when he hands over the kingdom to God the Father after he has destroyed all dominion, authority and power. For he must reign until he has put all his enemies under his feet. The last enemy to be destroyed is death. For he "has put everything under his feet."

In 1 Corinthians 15, Paul again blends Jesus as the kingly Messiah with Jesus as the eternal Son, but in this case he does so in a quite different and remarkable way. In the second phase of his argument with the believers in Corinth as to the certainty of their own future *bodily* resurrection, he asserts that with the coming of Christ himself, "the end will come, when [Christ] hands over the kingdom to God the Father" (v. 24).

The thrust of the passage has to do with the *eschaton*, the end, when the Son turns over his rule to the Father. Paul affirms that everything is already under his rule; indeed, he continues, the heavenly Messiah must rule until all his enemies are subdued, including especially the final enemy, death. In so arguing, Paul merges two texts that had long been understood as messianic. The exalted Messiah must reign on high until all his enemies are "a footstool for [his] feet" (Ps. 110:1), and this is because, as the Apostle quotes language of an earlier Psalm, God "has put everything under [the Son's] feet" (Ps. 8:6). Thus when the currently reigning messianic Son has—by resurrection to new life—destroyed the final enemy, death itself, that marks the end of the Son's messianic functions. With that Christ returns to his prior "role" as eternal Son.

Colossians 1:13–17

For [God] has rescued us from the dominion of darkness and brought us into the kingdom of the Son he loves, in whom we have redemption, the forgiveness of sins. The Son is the image of the invisible God, the firstborn over all creation. For in him all things were created: things in heaven and on earth, visible and invisible, whether thrones or powers or rulers or authorities; all things have been created through him and for him. He is before all things and in him all things hold together.

We turn, finally, to one of the Apostle's finest moments, the thanksgiving-turned-narrative at the beginning of his letter to the believers in Colossae. In this grand affirmation, Paul refers to the One who had redeemed these believers as "the Son [God] loves" and to their redemption as being brought into "the kingdom of the Son" (Col. 1:13). It is easy to see that much of this language has its roots in Israel's story: redemption into a kingdom ruled by God's Son. But when we come to the end of this brief narrative, even though Paul is still echoing Old Testament language about the Son's relationship to the Father, his concern now moves far beyond the Old Testament story to eternal verities. This Son preexisted with the Father, whose image he bears; this Son has the rights of primogeniture with regard to the whole created order, and that is because this Son is both the agent and the goal of the whole created order. Moreover, this Son is the head over all powers for the sake of his body (the redeemed ones), of whom he is also the head from which all the forces of life are drawn. The Son is thus both redeemer and creator of the new creation.

Conclusion

As we have seen in this chapter, Paul was able to hold both dimensions of his Son of God Christology in tension. First, Paul holds that the eternal

Son entered our history in the role of the messianic Son, becoming incarnate so as to redeem us. This view in turn leads to the second—and, for Paul, the ultimate—dimension of what it means for Jesus to be the Jewish Messiah: Jesus is none other than the eternal Son of God, who became incarnate not only to redeem fallen, broken humanity but also (especially) to reveal the eternal One, to reveal God's person and character. We take up this second dimension of Jewish messianism more fully in the next chapter.

7

Jesus as the Eternal Son of God

I n this chapter we examine the central matter of the entire Christian faith: that in a context of Jewish messianic expectations, where Israel's king was occasionally referred to as "God's son," the risen Lord, Jesus Christ, had come to be understood by those closest to him as the *eternal* Son of God. At some point early on they became certain that Jesus was the Son of God incarnate—fully human, both physically and mentally, while at the same time fully divine.[1] In Paul's letters as well as the rest of the New Testament, Jesus's true humanity is given full expression by way of the Spirit of God, whom early believers came to speak of as the Holy Spirit, who likewise enabled them to recognize the risen one as the incarnate one.

Below we begin with an overview of the data from Paul's letters and then examine these data under five different but related categories: the Son of God as Savior, as Son of the Father, as redeemer, as God's image-bearer, and as creator.

1. As I would often remind students as a way of helping them get this point, the Son of God wore diapers (or the first-century equivalent thereof).

Jesus as the Preexistent, Eternal Son of God: The Data

A basic issue for all readers of Paul's letters is how to understand the Apostle's designation of Jesus as "the Son of God," especially with regard to how he perceived the relationship of the Son to the Father. Here at the outset I offer an overview of the extent and nature of the various data to aid the reader.

1. Paul refers to Christ as *Son* seventeen times, sixteen of which are directly qualified in relationship to God (either "of God," "his," or "his own"). All of these appear in nine of his ten letters to churches (Philemon is the single exception). The only instance where a qualifier does not occur is at the conclusion of a paragraph in his argument with the Corinthians about the resurrection of the dead (1 Cor. 15:28). In this case, however, the intensive "the Son *himself*" takes the reader back to a middle sentence in the paragraph, where Paul says that the end will come when Christ "hands over the kingdom to God *the Father*" (v. 24). To be sure, this latter phrase has turned out to be quite ambiguous for later readers, regarding whether Paul intended "to his God and Father" or "to God, even the Father." But in either case, Paul's language implies sonship on the part of Christ himself.

2. In Paul's ten letters to churches—now including Philemon, which, as the salutation in v. 2 makes certain, was intended to be read aloud to all the believers in Colossae—Paul refers to God as "Father" thirty times, plus three more in the later Pastoral Epistles (1 and 2 Timothy and Titus), which are addressed to individuals rather than to churches. Apart from two passages, one early (1 Cor. 15:23–28) and one later (Col. 1:12–13), "Son" and "Father" do not occur in the same sentence or clause; in these two exceptions Paul's mention of the Son is separated from mention of the Father by at least twenty-six words. Thus Paul regularly refers to Jesus as "the Son of God" or "his [God's] Son" but never *explicitly* as the Son of *the Father*, even though it is arguable that such a construct might have been intended in one or more instances.

3. Of the thirty appearances of "Father," twenty-three occur in the combination "God and Father," eleven of which are qualified by "our"

("our God and Father"). Most likely this locution means something bordering on "our God, namely, the Father" or "our God, even the Father"—who is *our* Father precisely because he is "Father" of the "Son" who was sent to redeem us as God's children so as to re-create us back into the divine image.

4. Of the remaining twelve instances of the combination of "God and Father," three are qualified by "of our Lord, Jesus Christ" (2 Cor. 1:3; 11:31; Eph. 1:3), while the same combination also occurs once in Colossians (1:3) without the conjunction *kai* ("and" or "even"). Moreover, it seems most likely that the appositional use in this passage (i.e., "thanks be to God, the Father of our Lord, Jesus Christ") serves as the clue that in the other occurrences the phrase "the God and Father" is also appositional (= "God, even the Father" or "the God who is Father in relationship to the Son").

The Gospels bear clear witness to the origin in early Christian communities of speaking both about and directly to God as "Father," a practice continued in a thoroughgoing way by Paul. This in itself was an especially radical thing to do since, in the Jewish community in which Paul had been raised, God's name, Yahweh, was not often spoken aloud lest it be "taken in vain." Thus in their public reading of the Jewish Bible this community regularly substituted *Adonai* ("the Lord") where the divine name occurred, a phenomenon still carried on in contemporary English versions. That these early followers of Jesus would either address or talk about Yahweh in this matter-of-fact way must have been especially off-putting to contemporary Jewish communities and may very likely account for Saul of Tarsus's ambition to rid the world of such "heretics."

5. Emphasis on the relational aspect of the Son to the Father occurs in four instances. Two of these are expressed with the adjective "beloved" (Col. 1:13; Eph. 1:6) and the other two with the Greek reflexive pronoun, where it serves as an intensive (= "his own"; Rom. 8:3, 32). In Romans 8:32, Paul is very likely echoing the unique sonship of Isaac in the long narrative where Abraham is tested regarding his willingness to give up his "only" son sacrificially to God (Gen. 22:1–19).

What emerges from these data is that Christ as "Son of God" occurs in contexts that have to do with his relationship both to believers as their Savior and to God the Father. We turn now to examine in some detail both the affirmations and the assumptions Paul makes regarding these two dimensions of the Son's relationships.

The Son of God as Savior

When speaking of human redemption, Paul uses "Son of God" language in at least three kinds of settings. First, as noted above—and not surprisingly—Son of God language emerges when Paul reflects on Christ's present reign as king. This becomes especially clear from a careful reading of two key moments of affirmation, one quite early (1 Cor. 15:22–25) and the other somewhat later (Col. 1:13–15). Although there are not more of these moments in Paul's letters, the very presuppositional way the affirmations in these passages are expressed (nearly a decade apart) is especially noteworthy. Here again is something Paul is not arguing *for* but arguing *from* as a point of departure to stress some other matter. Especially in the earlier passage the Son is assumed presently to reign and to do so until the final enemy, Death, is destroyed and all things are restored to their prefallen, eternal destiny.

Second, Paul often writes of Christ as "Son of God" when he reflects on what it means for the redeemed to be in relationship with the eternal God as Father. This comes out especially in the twin passages in his letters to the Galatians and the Romans (Gal. 4:4–7; Rom. 8:14–18). In writing to the believers in Galatia, he tells them that human redemption is the direct result of God sending forth his Son and that the evidence of that redemption for believers lies with his sending forth the Spirit of his Son into our hearts whereby we use the Son's own language, *Abba*, thus indicating that we ourselves are God's children and thus heirs. Here especially the reality of Christ as the messianic and eternal Son of God merges in Paul's thinking. The Son who was sent into the world to redeem the lost does so in the context of the basic biblical story (born under the law). But the story works precisely because the redeemer is the *eternal* Son of God and thus a fully divine Savior. In an especially significant moment in his letter of friendship to the believers in Philippi, he puts it plainly. It was the one who was eternally in the form of God, and thus equal with God and fully divine, whose humble obedience to his Father in his incarnation led to his death on a cross (Phil. 2:6–8). As Richard Bauckham rightly recognizes, "Christology may not isolate Jesus' mission from his being. A purely functional Christology of God's action in Jesus' mission is inadequate, for his mission is rooted in his being the Son in his personal intimacy with the Father."[2]

This understanding of salvation—that we have become God's children through redemption by God's Son—is what lies behind Paul's utter devotion to Christ the Son, which eventually finds clear expression in Paul's letter to the Galatians: "The life I now live in the body, I live by faith in the Son of God, who loved me and gave himself for me" (Gal. 2:20). Here the emphasis is on the Son's love as demonstrated in his redeeming sacrifice, but it is also reflected in a much more relational way in the four passages where Paul speaks of God as "the Father of our Lord, Jesus Christ" (2 Cor. 1:3; 11:31; Col. 1:3; Eph. 1:3). The coming of the Son forever radicalized Paul's understanding of God, who is now blessed not in the language of Jewish transcendentalism—that is, blessed for his attributes of power and glory and otherness—but rather is blessed as the *Father of our Lord, Jesus Christ*, the God whom we now know through his Son. And it is this Son who came among us in sacrificial love so as to redeem and re-create us into the divine image in which humanity was originally created.

Third, Paul reflects a Son of God Christology when he considers our redemption in terms of the new creation. The children of Adam, who bear the image of their fallen forebear, are now being transformed back into God's own image, the image that in humanity has been thoroughly tarnished by the fall. This transformation is effected by the Son, who, on the one hand, himself perfectly bears that image ("the gospel that displays the glory of Christ, who is the image of God" [2 Cor. 4:4]), and who, on the other hand, also bears the true, perfect image of our humanity ("those God foreknew he also predestined to be conformed to the image of his

2. Richard Bauckham, "The Sonship of the Historical Jesus in Christology," in *The Historical Jesus*, vol. 3, *Jesus' Mission, Death, and Resurrection*, edited by Craig A. Evans (London: Routledge, 2004), 114.

Son" [Rom. 8:29]). Through the Son we are ever being transformed into the image of the eternal God as we are being shaped into the image of the Son, the one perfect human, who most truly bore the image of God because he was in fact God living a truly human life among us—but without sin.

Indeed, Son of God Christology frames the whole of a well-known and greatly loved passage in the middle of Paul's letter to the believers in Rome having to do with every believer's "life in the Spirit" (Rom. 8). The narrative begins with "God . . . sending his own Son in the likeness of sinful flesh" in order to condemn the sin that dwells in us all (Rom. 8:3). It is picked up again at the beginning of the application (vv. 14–17), whereby the Spirit of the Son brings about our adoption as "sons," the same Spirit who bears witness with our spirits that we are indeed God's children, and if children then heirs of God as joint heirs with Christ the Son.

Toward the end of this remarkable recital of life in and through the Spirit, the final purpose of God's redemptive work through Christ is expressed in terms of our being conformed into the Son's image, "that he might be the firstborn among many brothers and sisters" (Rom. 8:29). This is then followed with echoes of the story of Abraham and Isaac from the Genesis narrative (cf. Gen. 22), where Paul returns to the theme of God redeeming us through the gift of his Son: "He . . . did not spare his own Son, but gave him up for us all" (Rom. 8:32).

As is seen in these three moments in Paul's letters, Paul's Son of God Christology, with its roots deep in Israel's story, finds its grand expression in human redemption that transforms the redeemed into "sons" (as "children") and thus heirs of God. No wonder, then, when Paul bursts into doxology, it is expressed in terms of the God who is now known as the Father of our Lord, Jesus Christ, the eternal Son. For Paul, there is neither an attempt to persuade (the Colossians passage, for example, flows out of the thanksgiving) nor a need to call attention to the source of this language and imagery. Rather, this kind of expression simply flows out of Paul, very often as a basic assumption from which to argue for something else. And inherent to his affirmation of Jesus as the Son of God is that Jesus is the kingly Messiah, who redeems his people through a sacrificial death and subsequent resurrection. No human could ever have—or even wanted to have—created such an unlikely story. Surely the eternal God alone is so wise as to do something that on the surface would seem so foolish!

The Son of the Father

The above discussion has drawn out the *christological* implications that emerge in Paul's primarily *soteriological* concerns. As we've noticed before, we learn about Paul's understanding of the *person* of Christ primarily in contexts where he is speaking about the *work* of Christ as our redeemer. Looking more closely at Paul's language, then, we can see hints of the *eternal* Son's relationship to God the Father, an understanding that is embedded in several of these soteriological moments. These in turn account for Paul's thoroughgoing Christ devotion.

The Abba-*cry*

GALATIANS 4:6
Because *you* are his sons, God sent the Spirit of his Son into *our* hearts, the Spirit who calls out, "*Abba*, Father."

ROMANS 8:15
The Spirit you received brought about *your* adoption to sonship. And by him *we* cry, "*Abba*, Father."

One can scarcely minimize the christological significance of Paul's appeal to the use of the *Abba*-cry as evidence that the believers in Galatia and Rome are themselves God's children through the gift of the Spirit. At issue in both cases is that the believers do not need to observe Torah. But what must not be overlooked is the significance this has for Paul's understanding of Christ as Son of God—and especially noteworthy is the ungrammatical shift from "you" to "our" or "we" in both of these moments of reminder.

Paul makes a considerable point that the cry comes from human hearts because God the Father sent the Spirit *of his Son* into *our* hearts, thus eliciting the cry. Just as the Son was sent into the world to effect redemption, so the Spirit of the Son was sent into the world to effect redemption, and the Spirit of the Son has been sent into the hearts of believers to effect the experienced realization of that redemption. We will discuss the trinitarian nature of Paul's theology at greater length in the concluding chapter, but for now we can note that not only is the christological dimension of these twin affirmations considerable, but so also is the inherent triune character of God implied by such bold statements. Along with Paul's three clearly triadic affirmations (1 Cor. 12:4–6; 2 Cor. 13:14; Rom. 8:14–16), this passage also lies at the roots of all later trinitarian articulations, long before those articulations needed to be thought through, discussed, and finally understood to be basic to all truly Christian faith.[3]

There can be little question that this *Abba*-cry was retained in the early believing community—and continued to be used several decades later in the Greek-speaking communities—because Jesus himself prayed thus and so taught his followers to pray. However one might view the significance of this prayer for the earthly Jesus, these two passages in Paul's letters demonstrate that he understood it as the earthly prayer of the eternal Son of God. They are both Son of God passages, and one does not need to move toward spiritual sentimentality to recognize that such usage by the eternal Son (see Mark 14:36) points to a relational understanding of the Son with the Father.

Thus the very way Paul speaks of the *Abba*-cry points to an understanding of the risen Jesus as the Son of God that moves well beyond a mere matter of title. What becomes even more explicit in the Gospel of John is inherently present much earlier in Paul. Indeed, Pauline usage is very much in keeping with the Son of God Christology that appears in 1 John, even though the latter's concern is explicitly related to some who are "denying" the Son of God (1 John 2:22–23), which is later explicated in terms of their denying the reality of the incarnation.

The Echoes of Abraham and Isaac

ROMANS 8:3

For what the law was powerless to do . . . God did by sending *his own* son . . . to be a sin offering.

ROMANS 8:32

He who did not spare *his own* Son, but gave him up for us all . . .

---

3. Moreover, without trying to do so, Paul at this point spells the death knell to every form of "binitarian" theology, either assumed or articulated explicitly by groups such as the Mormons—whose denial of the Spirit as a "person" puts them outside the historic orthodox Christian faith.

Colossians 1:13

For he has rescued us from the dominion of darkness and brought us into the kingdom of the Son he loves.

Genesis 22:2

Take your son, your *only son*, whom you love . . . and . . . sacrifice him there.

Genesis 22:12

Now I know that you fear God, because you have not withheld from me your son, *your only* son.

The relational understanding of Jesus as the eternal Son of God emerges in Paul in his several echoes of the narrative of Abraham and Isaac in Genesis. This echo appears first in the strong affirmations of the believers' confidence in Romans 8. As noted above, this entire passage is both framed and carried along by a strong Son of God Christology. The frame occurs at the beginning (v. 3) and toward the end (v. 32) of this extraordinary moment in Paul's letters.

Here only in the corpus Paul emphasizes that God sent his "own" Son to effect redemption. This is then picked up toward the end with language taken directly out of the Genesis narrative, that "God spared not his 'own' Son," just as Abraham had been willing to do with his own son—even though this language is not used in the Genesis narrative. Paul's use of "own" (both the reflexive pronoun in v. 3 and the intensive in v. 32) is an instance of a rabbinic understanding of the Genesis narrative. For what God was asking Abraham to do was to sacrifice his "own" son in the sense that he was the special son of promise. In a moment of inspired insight Paul recognizes that the Son whom the Father both sent into the world and then offered up as a sacrifice for all was similarly and uniquely God's *own* Son.

This same background should be kept in mind when Paul refers to the "Son [God] loves" (Col. 1:13; cf. Eph. 1:6), since this is the language used in the Septuagint to refer to Isaac in Genesis, where the unique position of Isaac is emphasized: "Take your son, the beloved one, whom you love" (Gen. 22:2 LXX). It is not simply theological insight but theological reality that leads Paul in Romans 8 to refer to the Father "sparing not his 'only' Son" so as to effect eternal redemption for all others who will become his *sons* (= children, vv. 14 and 17).

These echoes push us beyond a merely positional understanding of the eternal Son of God to a relational one. It is *this* Son, the one who is eternally with the Father, the one whom the Father sent "in the likeness of our sinful flesh" (Rom. 8:3), the one whom he "gave . . . up for us all" (v. 32). Even though Paul does not emphasize the relational aspect of the Son to the Father, the language itself pushes the reader to think in these terms.

The Son of God as Redeemer

GALATIANS 2:20

I have been crucified with Christ and I no longer live, but Christ lives in me. The life I now live in the body, I live by faith in the Son of God, who loved me and gave himself for me.

We turn finally to a very personal—and very rare—expression of Paul's own relationship to the Son of God in his letter to the Galatians. Here in Galatians 2:20 Paul understands the divine nature and activity between the Father and the Son to be thoroughly interchangeable, for he describes a total transfer of the Father's activity to the Son. Most often Paul expresses the Savior's death on our behalf as evidence for, and the outflow of, God the Father's love for fallen humanity, who are in enmity against God. This is especially true of the Apostle's more theologically reflective narrative in Romans 5:6–8 and more poignantly later in the same letter when he writes: "[God] . . . did not spare his own Son, but gave him up for us all" (8:32). But in his earlier letter to the believers in Galatia, in a sudden outburst about Christ's death, this truth is expressed in an altogether personal way. Thus it is "the Son of God" himself who "loved *me*"; and likewise it is the Son of God who "gave himself up for *me.*" It is this same Son whom the Father *sent* into the world to redeem it (Gal. 4:4). This rare moment is especially personal and relational, and lying behind it is an understanding of the Son and the Father that is likewise personal and relational. This leads us next to those moments in Paul's letters where he identifies the Son as the one who in his incarnation became the ultimate divine image-bearer.

The Son as God's Image-Bearer

2 CORINTHIANS 4:4

The light of the gospel . . . displays the glory of Christ, who is the image of God.

ROMANS 8:29

Those God foreknew he also predestined to be conformed to the image of his Son.

COLOSSIANS 1:13, 15

For [God] has . . . brought us into the kingdom of the Son he loves . . . [who] is the image of the invisible God, the firstborn over all creation.

As was discussed in chapter 2, one of the more remarkable twists in New Testament scholarship was the identification of God's "image" with personified Wisdom, when Paul himself uses the term primarily of Christ as God's *Son*. We return to "image" language here to point out its significance for Paul's basic understanding of the relationship of the Son with the Father. Paul's emphasis with regard to this usage goes in both directions: the Son as the perfect divine image-bearer *in his humanity* and the Son as, first of all, the divine Son *of the Father*, whose image he perfectly bears. Here is the ultimate expression of the old adage, "Like Father, like Son." In the two earlier "image" passages (2 Cor. 4:4; Rom. 8:29), the emphasis is on Christ bearing the divine image as such, while in the context of the later passage, Christ is identified as "the Son [the Father] loves" (Col. 1:13).

The Son of God as Creator

Finally, we turn again briefly to the twin christological passages discussed in chapter 2 (1 Cor. 8:6; Col. 1:15–20) in order to observe how Paul not only presupposes the preexistence of the Son but also emphasizes Christ's prior role in *creation* before speaking of his role in redemption. The basic story is expressed in poetic shorthand in the letter to the Corinthians. The one *Theos* (God) of the Jewish Shema is now identified as "the Father," who is the *source* and *goal* of both creation and redemption. The one

Kyrios (Lord) of the Shema is Jesus Christ (the Son of the Father), who is the divine agent of both creation and redemption. Although Christ is not specified as Son in this passage, it is presupposed by Paul's identification of God as Father. Paul makes clear that the one Lord, Christ the Son, was eternally preexistent with the Father and was his copartner in both creation and redemption. If the Father is the *source* and *goal* of all things, the Son is the *divine agent* of all things, including creation itself.

This picture is described even more explicitly and thoroughly in the Colossians passage. In writing to the believers in Colossae, Paul turns from the story of redemption (Col. 1:12–14) to the story of creation (vv. 15–17)—and in that order. He begins by specifically identifying the Son as the one who in his incarnation bore the Father's image and holds all the rights of primogeniture. The Son has these rights precisely because he is the one through whom and for whom and by whom all things were created. The expansive nature of this passage can be attributed primarily to Paul's desire to put "the powers" in their rightful place, as both created by the Son and thus ultimately subservient to him. And as we noted in chapter 5, the Son is the one who is currently re-creating fallen humanity back into the divine image as the *beginning* of the new creation (v. 18)—an image he alone has perfectly borne (3:10–11).

Paul's Son of God Christology is his way of expressing not only the relationship of Christ to God the Father but also Christ's eternal preexistence, including his role in both the original creation and the new creation. As Son of God he bears the image of the Father in his humanity, and as Son of God he is re-creating a people of God into the divine image. As my Pentecostal heritage in me wants to exclaim, praise be to the eternal God!

Conclusion: The Question of Origins

By way of conclusion we turn finally to the question of origins: Where did Paul come by his understanding of Christ as the messianic Son of God who at the same time is the eternal Son? Raising the question of the source of Paul's *understanding* is, of course, different than questioning the *reality* behind that understanding. Moreover, Paul himself indicates that the origin of the *language* "Son of God" is to be found in a Jewish messianism that traces its roots back to the Davidic covenant, so neither is the question with the *terminology* itself, which lay ready at hand with Jewish end-time expectations that a greater David would appear and redeem his people from their present bondage. Rather, the question of origins has to do with how the *messianic* Son came to be identified with the *eternal* Son, who preexisted in the form of God and is thus equal with God (Phil. 2:6). There are three possible explanations, which we treat in turn.

First, it is possible that its origins for Paul can be traced back to his encounter with the risen and exalted Lord himself. This is the position taken by many based, unfortunately, on the untenable grounds of a mistaken reading of Galatians 1:15–16. There are simply no exegetical grounds—especially within the Pauline corpus—for reading Paul's plain grammar that the Son was "revealed *in* me" as though Paul really intended "revealed *to* me." As we discussed in chapter 5, Paul intended his own conversion to be a place of revelation for others—that in his own conversion from a Christ hater to a Christ devotee others could see Christ at work in the world. But one does not need this text in order to surmise that Paul's encounter with the risen Christ may have led him finally to understand Christ to have been the preexistent Son. I tend to agree with this possibility, even though there is no expressed evidence in Paul's letters for believing it to be so.

Second, some have argued that the answer lies with Jewish Wisdom. But as we argued in chapter 2, there is neither exegetical, linguistic, theological, nor historical grounds for the origins to lie here. This explanation requires either downplaying or denying the Son of God motif in the key passages, especially in the crucial affirmations that get front-page coverage in his letter to the believers in Colossae (Col. 1:13–17). This explanation both misrepresents the Wisdom tradition and reads into Paul something that the Apostle himself could not possibly have understood.

Third, Paul offers a possibility, through his use of the Aramaic *Abba* as an address to God the Father, that some form of Son of God Christology existed in the Aramaic Christian community before Paul became a believer. In this case, Paul's understanding of Christ as preexistent Son very likely had its origins in the community that preceded him. Why else would he, in two different letters to Greek-speaking communities of faith, have used this Aramaic near equivalent of our English "Daddy" as basic evidence that the Spirit of God the Father indwells the believer (Gal. 4:6; Rom. 8:15)?

But in the end it must be admitted that we simply do not know for certain where Paul came by his understanding of Christ as the preexistent eternal Son of God. I am attracted to the suggestion by Martin Hengel, who concludes on the basis of careful analysis of the available evidence, that "this development in christology [including *Kyrios* Christology] progressed *in a very short time*."[4] Citing *Barnabas* 6:13 ("Behold I make the last things as the first things"), Hengel extrapolates the possibility that such a view should also be seen in reverse: that the first things must be viewed in light of the last things. In his words, "the beginning *had* to be illuminated by the end."[5]

However an understanding of the preexistence of the Son of God arose in the earliest communities—whether by revelation, remembrance of Jesus, or thoughtful reflection—the reality exists in Paul in a thoroughly presuppositional way. Together with his *Kyrios* Christology discussed in part 4, his Son of God Christology both presupposes and expresses the kind of high Christology that finds very open, articulate expression in the Gospel of John. To be sure, their ways of expressing it are somewhat different; nonetheless, Paul and John are on the same christological page in the story, and in Paul's case he shares this high Christology with the recipients of his letters. As we have seen in part 3, whatever else may be true about Paul's Christian worldview, Son of God Christology is not peripheral to his theological enterprise. It is a crucially essential part that helps to make sense of the rest.

---

4. Martin Hengel, *The Son of God: The Origins of Christology and the History of Jewish-Hellenistic Religion* (Philadelphia: Fortress, 1976), 77; italics in the original.

5. Ibid., 69; italics in the original.

The Jewish Messiah
and Exalted Lord

Part 4 is devoted to the most significant of the christological motifs in Paul's letters and thus to the absolute heart of his Christology: Jesus as *Kyrios* (Lord). Although this title occurs less frequently than the title-turned-name *Christos* (Christ), there is good reason for this. In Paul's letters the name-turned-title *Kyrios* functions *only* as a title, whereas *Christos* frequently functions as both name and title. Even so, the *Kyrios* title predominates in Paul's earliest two letters (1 and 2 Thessalonians) as well as in the final one in the church corpus (Philippians) and in the Pastoral Letters (2 Timothy). Indeed, it plays a major role in all but two of his letters (2 Corinthians and Galatians).

Moreover, as noted in part 3, even though *Christos* is Paul's most frequent referent to Jesus, a little over half of these references stand alone as either subject or object in a sentence, whereas two-thirds of Paul's references to Jesus as "Lord" stand alone. These numbers themselves tell part of the story. For Paul, "Jesus" was a name. "Christ," however, began

117

as a title (Jesus the Christ = the Messiah), though eventually it too became very close to functioning as a name. Hence, even if unconsciously in most instances, the Apostle regularly refers to our Lord in terms of the *name* Jesus and the *title* Lord and with the *function* of Christ (= Messiah).

Especially noteworthy is that in the sixty-five instances where all three names/titles appear together, the title "the Lord" appears only in the first or last position—that is, either "the Lord, Jesus Christ [or 'Christ Jesus']" or "Jesus Christ [or 'Christ Jesus'], the Lord." This provides evidence that for Paul, *Kyrios* functioned exclusively as a title, even though its origins were in the divine name. For this reason, I have altered the NIV translation slightly by inserting a comma to set off "the Lord" from "Jesus Christ" or "Christ Jesus."

The significance of this name-turned-title for Paul can hardly be overstated. It is the way he begins every letter ("the Lord, Jesus Christ," i.e., "the Lord, namely, Jesus the Messiah") and is always used in conjunction with either "God the Father" or "God our Father." It is the language of the earliest Christian communities, who in Aramaic prayed *Marana tha* ("Come, Lord"; 1 Cor. 16:22). Moreover, it is the language Paul uses of his Damascus road experience: "Have I not seen Jesus our Lord?" (1 Cor. 9:1). Finally, it is the primary confession of those who become believers and thus followers of the risen one: "the Lord is Jesus [Christ]" (1 Cor. 12:3; Rom. 10:9; Phil. 2:11).

In this final part of the book, we first examine the ways Paul adapts the *divine name* from the Old Testament and transfers it to a title for Christ (chap. 8). We then discuss how Paul transfers the *divine roles* of Israel's Lord (Yahweh) to Christ, including his many intertextual echoes from Old Testament passages (chap. 9). And finally we unpack the many passages where Paul transfers the *divine prerogatives* of Israel's God to the Lord, Jesus Christ (chap. 10).

8

Paul's Use of the "Name" of the Lord

The purpose of this chapter is to pursue the theological undergirding of the name-turned-title "Lord," since—similar to Paul's use of "Son of God" (see chap. 7)—the christological implications of this usage are considerable. The significance of this language is so great that the reader is inevitably led to an understanding of Christ that can be explained only in terms of full deity, of a kind similar to that found in John's Gospel and in Hebrews with the descriptor "Son." Indeed, this usage especially requires one to indulge in theology, like it or not. This is because (1) the risen Lord shares every kind of divine prerogative with God the Father apart from "initiating" the saving event itself, but he does so (2) within the context of absolute monotheism and at the same time (3) in his redemptive and mediatorial roles always with God the Father as the first or last word.

The data of the present chapter, therefore, would seem to demand that one either give up monotheism (which is what Paul will *not* do) or do as the later church did as the result of the writings of Paul, John, and the author of Hebrews: find a way to understand and speak of the *One* God as triune—as Father, Son, and Holy Spirit. All contemporary scholarship that promotes what the early church understood as unorthodox, or "heresy"—namely, to subordinate the Son and the Spirit to the

Father—is thoroughly unbiblical and thus lies outside the parameters of the orthodox Christian faith. We use the adjective "unorthodox" in the sense that such views promote what seems to be a considerable misunderstanding of Paul's writings, which the early church included as part of its Holy Scriptures.

The title "Lord"—as with the term "Son of God" discussed in part 3—is laden with messianic implications. But in this case the implications have to do with the *eschatological* dimension of Christ as Messiah, where the messianic Lord—in "fulfillment" of a crucial moment in the Psalter (110:1)—is seated at the "right hand" of God, from which he will return to accompany his people into eternity. In the ancient world this imagery was used exclusively to indicate primacy of position in relation to a sovereign. As we'll see below, Paul takes up this language and applies it to the risen Lord, Jesus.

Jesus Christ, Exalted Messianic Lord

1 CORINTHIANS 9:1

Am I not free? Am I not an apostle? Have I not seen Jesus our Lord? Are you not the result of my work in the Lord?

The language Paul uses to describe his life-changing encounter with the risen Christ serves as a good starting point for our discussion. In a crucial moment in defense of his apostleship ("Am I not an apostle?"), Paul rhetorically asks the believers in Corinth a follow-up question as the first line of evidence of his apostleship: "Have I not seen Jesus our Lord?" (1 Cor. 9:1). Paul then returns to this encounter at a later point in the letter when referring to Christ's appearance to him after the ordinary time of resurrection appearances had passed: "he appeared to me also, as to one abnormally born" (15:8). Although it is possible (but unlikely) that this latter imagery is a self-effacing reference to the Apostle's small stature, it is much more in keeping with what he indicates elsewhere to be his way of acknowledging that his encounter with Christ occurred some time after appearances of the risen Lord had ceased. But in either case Paul's point is clear: he has *seen* the risen Lord.

The Apostle's language in this passage indicates quite clearly that he did not think of his encounter with the Lord as a visionary experience of some kind. Rather, he considered it to be of the same kind as those encounters that the earliest disciples had experienced. The risen Christ "appeared to me also" (15:8), Paul writes in the same language he uses to describe Christ's appearances to the disciples—therefore suggesting that Christ appeared the same way. To be sure, Paul did have visionary experiences, as he reveals in a moment of "boasting" to the Corinthians (2 Cor. 12:1–5), but of these moments he refers not to "seeing" the Lord but to "hearing" heavenly things that cannot be expressed on earth below. Thus there can be little question as to Paul's own understanding of what happened. He asserts that he saw the Lord, even though this had clearly happened postascension and thus outside the normal time span of the other appearances. This encounter is further evidenced in Luke's condensed secondhand version of this commissioning in Paul's speech before Agrippa (Acts 26:12–18).

Paul's encounter with the risen Lord is where he first received his commission to serve as an apostle. That seems to be the intent of the juxtaposition of the three rhetorical questions that begin the somewhat discursive moment in an argument with the believers in Corinth. Clearly against their will, he absolutely prohibits their attending meals at the temples of idols (1 Cor. 8:10). So in response to their (anticipated) objections to this—that is, *Why can't we since the "gods" have no real existence?*—he unleashes a series of rhetorical questions that includes, "Am I not an apostle?" From what follows there can be little question that some of the Corinthians had a measure of doubt on this score. So Paul follows this question with the two primary kinds of evidence that substantiate his apostleship. He asks rhetorically, "Have I not seen Jesus our Lord?" In Paul's view, this is the first requirement for apostleship. It is uncertain whether the Corinthians themselves would have known this, but what he asserts is clear enough: he has *seen* and been commissioned by the Lord himself. For the Apostle this was the first standard of apostleship.

The next rhetorical question serves equally as substantial evidence: "Are you not the result of my work in the Lord?" From Paul's perspective, therefore, his apostleship was based on the two primary factors of (1) his having seen and been commissioned by the risen Lord and (2) his having founded communities of believers. This was for him especially true among gentiles, who by way of faith in Christ Jesus were part of God's newly formed people apart from adherence to the law. For the Apostle the inclusion of gentiles was clearly the eye-opener that lies behind his impassioned argument that the gentiles are not beholden to keep the law.

This tight series of rhetorical questions is undoubtedly compressed, but the basic realities are in place. At issue for us, therefore, in terms of Paul's Christology is where Paul came by this use of language, this calling the risen Jesus "Lord." The answer in part is that such language belonged to the earliest believers from the very beginning—well before Paul became one of them—as evidenced by the Aramaic-speaking community's prayer, *Marana tha* ("Come, Lord," 1 Cor. 16:22), perhaps in conjunction with the Lord's table. It seems likely that in keeping with others in the earliest community of believers, Paul had come to understand this new title for Jesus in light of Christ's own interpretation of a crucial moment in the Psalter, which had been passed down among them: "The Lord [= Yahweh] says to my lord [King David]: 'Sit at my right hand until I make your enemies a footstool for your feet'" (Ps. 110:1). For several reasons this had become a significant *messianic* text in Second Temple Judaism. It is the Old Testament passage most frequently cited or alluded to in the New Testament, including by Jesus himself in controversy with the Jewish leaders (e.g., Mark 12:35–37). Paul refers to it no less than four times in his preserved letters, which deserve examination here.

1 Corinthians 15:25–27

For [Christ] must reign until he has put all his enemies under his feet. The last enemy to be destroyed is death. For he "has put everything under his feet." Now when it says that "everything" has been put under him, it is clear that this does not include God himself, who put everything under Christ.

Romans 8:34

Who then is the one who condemns? No one. Christ Jesus who died—more than that, who was raised to life—is at the right hand of God and is also interceding for us.

Colossians 3:1

Set your hearts on things above, where Christ is, seated at the right hand of God.

Ephesians 1:19–23

That power is the same as the mighty strength [God] exerted when he raised Christ from the dead and seated him at his right hand in the heavenly realms, far above all rule and authority, power and dominion, and every name that is invoked, not only in the present age but also in the one to come. And God placed all things under his feet and appointed him to be head over everything for the church, which is his body, the fullness of him who fills everything in every way.

Psalm 110:1

The Lord [= Yahweh] says to my lord [= King David]: "Sit at my right hand until I make your enemies a footstool for your feet."

In his long argument with the Corinthians about the future *bodily* resurrection of believers, Paul brings forward this Davidic moment to speak of Christ's present reign, a reign that will last until the final enemy, death, is brought under his feet (1 Cor. 15:27). In Paul's context this refers to the time when those who have put their trust in Christ are raised from the dead. This usage has clear messianic implications since in the psalm he is alluding to, "the Lord" is the one who reigns on high (Ps. 110:1).

In his letter to the Roman believers, the allusion takes on the interesting dimension of reference to Christ's present ministry of heavenly intercession for those who are his (Rom. 8:34). Here Paul picks up in a larger metaphorical sense that the one at the right hand of a king was regularly recognized as having the most influence with the king. Thus, in his later letter to the believers in Colossae, the same allusion is used as a reference point regarding Christ's present position and is intended, as it was in his letter to the believers in Rome, to serve as both encouragement and exhortation (Col. 3:1). And finally, in what was most likely something of a circular letter to believers in the Roman province of Asia that ended up in the capital city of Ephesus, the same affirmation occurs in the opening thanksgiving and prayer (Eph. 1:19–23). Here, as in 1 Corinthians 15, the allusion to Psalm 110 is used to refer to Christ's present lordship over all the demonic powers (Eph. 1:20–21).

We can note three observations about Paul's references to the *risen Christ* as sitting "at the right hand" of God the Father. First, in none of these allusions does Paul use the title "Lord," the actual language of Psalm 110 as it appears in the Septuagint. Although this omission could be incidental, having to do in each case with the issue at hand, this phenomenon nonetheless also fits well with the Apostle's usage elsewhere, especially in light of our next point.

Second, although *Kyrios* occurs throughout the Septuagint as a translation of the divine name, Yahweh, into Greek, Paul uses this title *exclusively* for Christ. Thus, despite its regular appearance in his Greek Bible as the rendering for Yahweh, Paul does not use this noun as a reference to God the Father. He uses the term *Theos* exclusively for God—with only two possible exceptions: Romans 9:5 and Titus 2:13, each of which comes in his citations of the Greek Bible where the mention of God is not pertinent to the point of the citation as such.[1]

---

1. In both cases there is considerable ambiguity in the structure of Paul's Greek sentences. Both are brief, offhanded moments, and in both cases two (or three) different understandings are viable options of Paul's otherwise ambiguous Greek clauses. In the first instance, Rom. 9:5, the alternatives are given in the NIV footnote. Did Paul intend (a) "the Messiah, who is God over all, forever praised" (as in the text itself) or (b) "the Messiah, who is over all. God be forever praised" or (c) "the Messiah. God who is over all be forever praised"?

What speaks against the NIV rendering is the absolute uniqueness of such a way of speaking in the entire Pauline corpus. Why would Paul, in this singular instance, abandon his consistent usage of "God" as a referent to God the Father and of "Lord" as a referent to Christ? After all, the Apostle himself already has it "both ways," as it were, in his consistent use of the Septuagint translators' rendering of "Yahweh" as "Lord" and applying such moments to the risen Christ. This in itself should cause the translator in the present case to lean toward one of the two other options, which seem equally preferable.

The translational problem arises from the twofold reality that (a) Paul never elsewhere uses the Greek word *Theos* ("God") when he refers to Christ and that (b) the "substitute" *Kyrios* (= Yahweh) of the Septuagint is now used exclusively by Paul as a referent to Christ and never to God the Father. So even though Paul's grammar *could* go in another direction, his consistent use of *Kyrios* and *Theos* elsewhere to refer to Christ and God respectively should tip the scales decisively in this direction here.

This accounts for our departure from the NIV text in this singular instance, especially so in light of Paul's own strong affirmation that "*for us* there is but one God [*Theos*] the Father," and "there is but one Lord [*Kyrios*], Jesus Christ" (1 Cor. 8:6). And while Ralph Waldo Emerson's line that "foolish consistency is the hobgoblin of little minds" is often true, in this case Paul himself is so thoroughly consistent one would need especially strong evidence of any kind to imagine that Paul has here deviated, since his consistency is by no means "foolish."

Third, notwithstanding one or two early exceptions, Paul consistently uses the title *Kyrios* when referring either to Christ's present reign or anticipated coming. The primary exceptions occur when he refers to something said by Jesus (e.g., 1 Cor. 7:10, 12; 11:23; and possibly 1 Thess. 4:15). Thus "Jesus" or "Christ" but never "the Lord" died for us, though in Paul's earliest letter he does speak of the crucifixion as the killing of "the Lord, Jesus" (1 Thess. 2:14–15). In this single case, however, the clause seems to be deliberately full of irony (in their own ignorance of who he was and is, the people crucified the Lord of the universe!). Paul is reflecting on what his own people did: they had the Romans execute their Messiah, Jesus, whom God the Father would reinstate as Lord of all.

The other possible exception to Paul's consistent usage occurs in a quite indirect way in an important paragraph regarding Christ's role as the "firstfruits of those who have fallen asleep" (1 Cor. 15:20). At a crucial moment in his argument, where Paul is trying to convince the Corinthian believers of the future bodily resurrection of the dead, he uses the language of a messianic psalm (Ps. 110:1) to note that this will happen at "the end" when Christ hands over the kingdom to God the Father (1 Cor. 15:24). As part of that event Christ will "put everything under his feet" (v. 27). But here Paul's sentence has no expressed grammatical subject, therefore putting this apparent exception into an altogether different category as to whether the intended referent of the pronoun is Christ or God.

For Paul it is "Christ" (= the Messiah) who is "seated at the right hand of God," which very likely also reflects the intent of the psalmist.

The passage in Titus is equally ambiguous in terms of the actual structure of Paul's sentence. Did he intend, "the appearing and glory of our great God and Savior, Jesus Christ" or "the appearing and glory of our great God, even our Savior, Jesus Christ"? The problem in this case is further complicated by the fact that the Greek of the three Pastoral Epistles (1 and 2 Tim. and Titus) differs just enough from the other ten Pauline letters to have made them suspect as to authorship—a problem we prefer to resolve in terms of Paul's use of a different amanuensis who was also allowed a bit of freedom in the actual "writing" of the letter—and that is not to mention their unique nature as letters to individuals rather than to churches.

At any rate, the combination in both cases of the ambiguity of the Greek and Paul's otherwise absolute consistency in terms of usage should cause translators to favor Pauline consistency over a desire to affirm Christ's deity in this less than certain way. After all, that deity is writ large throughout the church corpus, and going the other route here seems especially difficult since it stands in considerable tension with Paul's earlier affirmation that "for us there is but one God, the Father, . . . and there is but one Lord, Jesus Christ" (1 Cor. 8:6).

Paul's use of the title "Lord," however, is quite unrelated to the messianic referent involved. Rather, "Lord" is the title by which Paul regularly and exclusively includes Christ in the divine identity.

Throughout the extant Pauline corpus, Paul remains singularly consistent with his use of *Kyrios* when citing or echoing the Septuagint. To be sure, he had come to this through his own tradition where, by way of substituting *Adonai* (= LORD) for Yahweh in oral readings, the Jewish community would never take the divine name in vain. Nonetheless, for Paul the designation "Lord"—which was first of all the Greek form of substitution for the divine name itself—becomes a title bestowed on Christ. Even though the title sometimes carries a degree of ambiguity because of its initial point of reference, for Paul it is used altogether as a title—exclusively with reference to Christ, the Son of God—and never as a name. To this matter we now turn.

The "Name" above Every Name

Five crucial affirmations offer us the clues to our theological understanding of this name-turned-title given to the risen Christ Jesus (1 Cor. 8:6; Phil. 2:9–11; Rom. 10:9–13; 1 Cor. 1:2; 2 Tim. 2:22). What is stated explicitly in these several moments of extraordinary affirmation serve as the presuppositional basis for our understanding of Paul's regular and consistent use of *Kyrios* with reference to Christ and therefore of his basic understanding of *who* Christ is. We treat each of these passages in turn.

Jesus, the Lord of the Shema

1 CORINTHIANS 8:6

For us there is but one God, the Father, from whom all things came and for whom we live; and there is but one Lord, Jesus Christ, through whom all things came and through whom we live.

Very early on in the extant Pauline corpus, Paul uses the fundamental expression of Jewish monotheism, the Shema ("Hear, O Israel, the LORD [= Yahweh] our God, the LORD [= Yahweh] is One"; Deut. 6:4), to include Christ in the identity of the one God. This moment was occasioned by some Corinthian believers who, in the name of *gnosis* (knowledge), had laid hold of this monotheistic reality so as to argue that, since there is only one God, the "gods" and "lords" of the pagan temples do not exist. Thus they had concluded that attendance at feasts in the environs of pagan temples should be a matter of indifference since there is no actual "god" in the temple.

In countering this gnosis of theirs, Paul first affirms the correctness of the basic theological presupposition, "there is but one God" (1 Cor. 8:6). But he vehemently rejects what they are doing with it, for two expressed reasons. First, such an action on the part of the so-called knowing ones plays havoc with other believers for whom Christ died but who cannot make these fine distinctions. But second, even more significant, they have misunderstood the true nature of the idol. Paul will eventually assert that even though these "gods" and "lords" do not exist as deities, the pagan temples in which the idols dwell are the habitations of *demons*. What is altogether impossible is for those who believe in Christ as Lord to eat at the Lord's table and also at the table of demons (10:13–22).[2]

But in his initial rejection of their reasoning, Paul does a most remarkable thing (1 Cor. 8:4–6). For the moment he acknowledges that for those who do not know the one and only God there are indeed "many

---

2. It is surely one of the unfortunate realities of many modern readers of Scripture, especially those in Western cultures, that demons are understood as only belonging to ancient mythology. But anyone with even minimal experience in so-called third-world settings knows that the *reality* of the satanic world is alive and well indeed. Only in our so-called educated Western settings has Satan so completely won the day! People in majority-world cultures are not so gullible as to be so thoroughly deceived by his cunning. The existence of demons is part and parcel of both their worldview and their experience.

Perhaps the even greater difficulty for later readers in a more democratic culture, where eating together is much more of a norm, is to appreciate what would have been the norm at the time of Paul's writing this letter. One need only to be reminded of the presentation on American public television of the British series *Upstairs Downstairs* to have a sense of how radical such cross-cultural eating would have been for the first recipients of this letter. It simply was not done.

Thus for Paul, and against all culturally defined standards, this was a crucial leveling of the playing field for followers of the crucified one. And later readers, raised and conditioned by more democratic eating habits in contemporary Western cultures, need at least to try to imagine the radical nature of what Paul here asserted. One can scarcely imagine the well-to-do householder sharing a table with *hoi polloi*, or commoners, yet for the Apostle this had become the crucial matter whereby all believers are acknowledged as sisters and brothers in the one divine family.

'gods' and many 'lords'" (v. 5). "Yet for us," he continues, there is only "one God" and only "one Lord" (v. 6). How Paul comes to this is one of the truly significant moments in early Christian theology. He divides the Shema itself into two parts, something available to him only in the Septuagint. In the Septuagint the Shema reads: "[the] *Lord* [= Yahweh] our God, [the] *Lord* is One." And because the risen Christ had "the name" Lord bestowed on him at his exaltation, Paul now does this truly remarkable thing: he applies the two words of the Shema, "God" and "Lord," to God the Father and Christ the Son respectively. What Paul here asserts is that the exalted Son of God is understood to be included in the divine identity, as the efficient *agent* of both creation and redemption ("through whom all things came"), of which God the Father is seen as the ultimate *source* and *goal*. Paul does this in a way that does not impinge on either the Corinthians' or our understanding of his basic monotheism. For the Apostle, when citing or echoing the Old Testament (where *Kyrios* = *Adonai* = Yahweh), *Kyrios* consistently and exclusively is applied to the risen Lord, Jesus. The clue as to *how* this came about is to be found in the next passage to be examined (Phil. 2:9–11).

But before we turn to Philippians, we need to call attention to what is said in the present affirmation about the one Lord: that he is both the *preexistent* divine agent of *creation* and the *incarnate* agent of human *redemption*. Since nothing further is made of creation in this immediate context, the affirmation may simply be nothing more than a typically Jewish affirmation about God vis-à-vis all other so-called gods and lords. But it is also possible, and even likely, that this affirmation about the one Lord as agent of creation prepares the way for a later affirmation in this letter (1 Cor. 10:26) at the beginning of the next section of the argument (10:23–11:1). Here Paul is expressly dealing with food *sold in the marketplace*, which is purchased to be eaten in one's own domicile. Thus it stands in considerable contrast to his earlier absolute prohibition against eating in the pagan temples.

Now believers are encouraged to "eat anything" available to them in the market (1 Cor. 10:25) since, in the words of an earlier psalm, "the earth is the Lord's, and everything in it" (v. 26; cf. Ps. 24:1). For Paul, the one Lord, Jesus Christ, who was the divine agent of creation in the first place, is the same Lord before whom every knee will eventually bow.

Thus Paul places Christ the Lord as the preexistent *agent* of creation, but he also sees him, with reference to Psalm 24, as the *Kyrios* to whom the whole of creation *belongs*. This is evidence of Paul's especially high Christology, which he simply assumes in his argument. By the time this letter was written (within two decades of the crucifixion and resurrection), this is now presuppositional language for which Paul does not even feel the need to argue.

The Bestowal of the Name

PHILIPPIANS 2:9–11

Therefore God exalted him to the highest place and gave him the name that is above every name, that at the name of Jesus every knee should bow, in heaven and on earth and under the earth, and every tongue confess that Jesus Christ is *Lord*, to the glory of God the Father.

In the grand christological passage in his letter to the believers in Philippi, Paul concludes his narrative of the essential Christ story by affirming God the Father's vindication of the Son—that the one who was *equal* with God (Phil. 2:6) demonstrated the real character of Godlikeness by the twofold act of pouring himself out, so as to become servant of all, and humbling himself in his obedient, sacrificial death on the cross (vv. 7–8). In the conclusion, divine vindication takes the form of God bestowing on Christ *the name*, which is identified as "above every name" (v. 9).

Any careful reading of this passage should make it quite clear that Paul's language can refer only to the divine name, which functions as a central feature of Israel's self-understanding. The name of Israel's God, *Yahweh*, first revealed to Moses at Horeb/Sinai (Exod. 3:1–6), was to serve as Israel's primary identity symbol. The Israelites were people of "the name," that is, of their God, Yahweh, who eventually chose Jerusalem as the place where they were to build a "temple for my Name" (1 Kings 5:5), and in whose "Name" all Israelites were to make and carry out their oaths.

In this crucial moment in the history of Christian theology, Paul asserts that this is the name that has been bestowed on the risen Christ at his exaltation. Now, however, the name is no longer reprised in its original Hebrew form, "Yahweh." Rather, by way of this happy accident of history, for Paul and the early church it appears singularly in its Greek expression, *Kyrios*. So the risen Christ is not Yahweh himself, who is always referred to by Paul as *God*. Rather, the preexistent *Son of God* returns by way of his resurrection to receive the honor of having bestowed on him the *substitute name* for God, which for Paul then becomes a *title* for Christ as "Lord"—and this "name" is now used by Paul exclusively for Christ and never for God the Father.

This was the reality already in place when Paul made his earlier assertion regarding the Shema in 1 Corinthians 8:6. And now, when writing to his beloved friends in Philippi, this usage is made altogether certain. Here Paul's intertextual use of the divine oath is expressed in the first person in a Yahweh oracle in Isaiah (45:18–24). Yahweh has sworn by his own name that "before me every knee will bow" (v. 23). In place of Isaiah's "before me," referring to Israel's one God, Yahweh, Paul now insists that the promise of every knee bowing before "him" and every tongue confessing "him" as God alone has been transferred to the risen and exalted Lord, Jesus Christ. And thus apparently not satisfied with just the text of Isaiah as it stands, Paul rather lavishly elaborates the "every knee" and "every tongue" to include all created beings: "in heaven, on earth, and under the earth" (Phil. 2:10).

For the Apostle there was coming a "day" when even the current Roman emperor, Nero Caesar, who was ultimately responsible for the present suffering of the believers in Philippi, would acknowledge the lordship of the Messiah. The final result is that the incarnate eternal One whom the empire had once tried to eliminate was part and parcel of the ultimate divine design. In what had by now come to be in typical fashion, here Paul clearly understands that God chose once more to take what the world would consider foolishness as his own way to "shame" those who consider themselves to be "the wise" (1 Cor. 1:27).

This passage in Philippians thus serves as a classic example of the transfer of a singularly divine prerogative—and thus of every kind of divine privilege—to the risen Lord, as demonstrated throughout the Pauline corpus. In Paul's repeated citations and intertextual use of the Septuagint he consistently identifies the *Kyrios* (= Yahweh) of the Septuagint with the risen Lord, Jesus Christ, whenever *Kyrios* is the reason for, or otherwise an important part of, the biblical citation.

This passage also has a singularly eschatological perspective to it. According to Paul this universal acknowledgment will take place at the end, the *eschaton*. We thus turn to our third significant text to point out that this phenomenon, the lordship of Christ, serves as the *entry point* for all who would embrace Christ as Savior and thus become part of the newly formed people of God.

Confessing the Name

ROMANS 10:9–13

If you declare with your mouth, "Jesus is Lord," and believe in your heart that God raised him from the dead, you will be saved. For it is with your heart that you believe and are justified, and it is with your mouth that you profess your faith and are saved. . . . For there is no difference between Jew and Gentile—the same Lord is Lord of all and richly blesses all who call on him, for "Everyone who calls on the name of the Lord will be saved" [Joel 2:32].

DEUTERONOMY 30:14

The word is very near you; it is in your mouth and in your heart so you may obey it.

In his letter to believers in Rome, the majority of whom he does not know personally, Paul argues that God is not finished with his ancient people Israel. Even though in the present time the newly formed people now very likely included more gentiles than Jews, Paul makes a typically bold move with regard to an important Old Testament passage with its promise of covenant renewal. At a key point in his argument in Romans 10, Paul applies the language of "mouth" and "heart" from an especially important moment in Deuteronomy (30:14), where Yahweh assures Israel that the word will be neither too difficult for them nor too distant from them. This, Paul says, is how Jew and gentile together become the one eschatological people of God: by confessing with the *mouth* that the Lord is Jesus and by believing with the *heart* that he is the risen (and thus exalted) one.

This juxtaposition of what is believed with the heart and confessed with the mouth is significant. What is believed is that God has raised the crucified Messiah from the dead and exalted him to the highest place, having bestowed on him the name (Phil. 2:9–11). Thus the *confession* with the mouth that Jesus is Lord is based on this prior *belief* with the heart that Christ, through his resurrection and exaltation, has assumed his present role as Lord of all. That the confession of the mouth refers to the same phenomenon as in the Philippians passage is made certain by the follow-up citation of the passage from Joel. There is no distinction between Jew and Greek on this matter, Paul says, because "everyone who calls on the name of the Lord will be saved" (Rom. 10:13; cf. Joel 2:32). Here again the Apostle has taken a very important eschatological text—as it appears in the Septuagint, where "the name of the Lord" refers specifically to the divine name Yahweh—and has applied it directly to the risen Christ. Thus the declaration of Jesus as "Lord" (Rom. 10:9)—which mirrors the eschatological confession of the name (Phil. 2:10–11)—is for Paul the way of entry into the new covenant people of God.

What happens both at the entry point and at the eschatological conclusion serves for Paul as a way to identify God's newly formed people. This usage further plays itself out in Paul's letters in a variety of other ways that reflect this total transfer to Christ of the "name" of Yahweh in its Greek form *Kyrios* ("Lord"). These early believers could have it both ways: keep the divine name Yahweh in place, but now in its Greek form, and transfer it to the risen Christ. The problem for us later readers in English is that "Christ" can stand alone as a name, although one may also refer to "the Christ," meaning "the Messiah." But that is not at all possible with *Kyrios*, which in English can never be a name but is always an identifying word, "*the* Lord." In translation, therefore, what could happen with a degree of subtlety in Greek is not possible in English. Hence for the English reader it is always a title, and never a name, an impoverishment in the otherwise richest and most flexible language in the Indo-European family of languages.

Calling on the Name

1 Corinthians 1:2

To the church of God in Corinth, to those sanctified in Christ Jesus and called to be his holy people, together with all those everywhere who call on the name of our Lord, Jesus Christ—their Lord and ours.

2 TIMOTHY 2:22

Pursue righteousness, faith, love, and peace, along with those who call on the Lord out of a pure heart.

The language of Joel 2:32, which we encounter in Romans 10:13, also occurs in two other places in the Pauline corpus, in both cases as a way to identify all of God's new covenant people. In Paul's first letter to the Corinthians, Joel's language appears in the salutation in an elaborated form, which was almost certainly intended to catch their attention (1 Cor. 1:2). Paul reminds the Corinthian believers that they belong to a much larger network of believers and therefore need to keep in step with that larger community. Thus he refers to "the church of God in Corinth" who have been "called to be his holy people [or 'saints']" along with "all those everywhere who call on the name of the Lord, Jesus Christ—their Lord and ours" (1 Cor. 1:2). With this one line Paul is able to offer three reminders: (1) that the Corinthian believers' conversion meant that they had now become a part of God's *holy* people (traditionally "saints"); (2) that in so doing they had joined a much wider network of believers, all of whom "call on the name of the Lord"; and (3) that they are thus under the lordship of the one on whom they call. Here, then, for Paul is the biblical language that emphasizes the universalizing aspect of the work of Christ and the Spirit.

In Paul's much later letter to Timothy, the Apostle's young disciple is urged to join with others who "call on the Lord out of a pure heart" (2 Tim. 2:22) and thus to live in keeping with the name on which they call. The command to Timothy is a clear pickup of the second "solid foundation" of the newly formed temple of God, and Timothy is thus encouraged first to remember that "the Lord knows those who are his" (v. 19)—echoing an affirmation made by Moses during the Korah rebellion (Num. 16:5).

But the second "foundation," Timothy is reminded, is that those who belong to the Lord—"everyone who confesses the name of the Lord" (echoing Isa. 26:13)—must "turn away from wickedness" (2 Tim. 2:19), clearly intending that Christlike behavior is assumed and thus expected of those who confess the name. Thus the name of the Lord, which was to be the identifying symbol of God's people Israel, has in each of these cases been transferred to the newly formed people of God, where "the Lord" whose "name" now identifies them is the risen and exalted Christ Jesus. And in keeping with what he regularly urges in his letters to churches, "those who call on [the name of] the Lord" (v. 22) are expected to conduct themselves in a way that will not bring shame on the name.

Other Matters Done in the Name of the Lord, Jesus

1 CORINTHIANS 6:11

But you were washed, you were sanctified, you were justified in the name of the Lord, Jesus Christ, and by the Spirit of our God.

2 THESSALONIANS 1:12

We pray this so that the name of our Lord, Jesus, may be glorified in you, and you in him.

COLOSSIANS 3:17

And whatever you do, whether in word or deed, do it all in the name of the Lord, Jesus, giving thanks to God the Father through him.

1 THESSALONIANS 5:27

I charge you before the Lord to have this letter read to all the brothers and sisters.

2 THESSALONIANS 3:6, 12

In the name of the Lord, Jesus Christ, we command you, brothers and sisters, to keep away from every believer who is idle and disruptive and does not live according to the teaching you received from us. . . . Such people we command and urge in the Lord, Jesus Christ, to settle down and earn the food they eat.

We conclude this chapter with this series of incidental moments in Paul's letters where in an offhanded way he appeals either to "the name of the Lord, Jesus," or simply to the Lord himself. A good place to begin is with the way he concludes his passionate disapproval of the two "brothers" in his first letter to the Corinthians, where one has defrauded another, who in turn has gone to the pagan courts to redress his grievances

(1 Cor. 6:1–11). Paul begins with a contrast to participating in sins of all kinds common to life in Roman Corinth, spelled out in vivid detail in verses 9 and 10. This is then followed with three significant metaphors for conversion, where Paul reminds the believers in that great city that they have been "washed," "sanctified," and "justified *in the name of the Lord, Jesus Christ*"—as well as "by the Spirit of our God" (1 Cor. 6:11).[3]

This fourth occurrence of the phrase "in the name of the Lord" in the letter (the most of any letter in the corpus) is most likely intended to serve as the believers' primary identity marker. Just as with Israel of old, who were identified as a people of the name, so with believers under the new covenant. At their conversion they call on the *name* of the Lord precisely because that is the name by which they are now to be identified. Thus the Lord, Jesus Christ, has for Paul now assumed a role that belonged exclusively to Yahweh in the Jewish tradition of which Paul had been—and still considers himself to be—a part.

Closely related to this usage is Paul's prayer for the Thessalonians in his second letter to them (2 Thess. 1:12). After a series of intertextual echoes in his thanksgiving, where Christ the Lord (= Yahweh) will mete out judgment on their opponents (echoing Isa. 66:4–6), Paul continues in this vein in his prayer for them (again echoing the same passage from Isaiah). What Paul desires for them is that by the way they live, "the *name of our Lord*, Jesus, *may be glorified* in you" (the italicized words are taken directly from Isa. 66:5). Thus not only are God's newly formed people to be identified as people of the name; they are urged also to live in a way that brings glory to that name—which picks up the theme of Christ being glorified in his people. As with the Isaiah passage, so too in the conclusion of Micah's great eschatological oracle (Mic. 4:1–5), the prophet contrasts God's future Israel with the surrounding nations who "walk in the name of their gods" (= live by the authority of and in keeping with their gods). Israel, Micah says, will do the same: "We will walk in the name of the LORD [Yahweh] our God for ever and ever" (v. 5). Even

---

3. With these verbs Paul covers the ground, as it were, of the entire experience of conversion. They have been "justified" as an act of God through Christ; they were "washed" by way of baptism, which signifies death, burial, and resurrection to newness of life; and they were "sanctified" in the sense of being set apart as God's newly formed holy people, to bear God's likeness in both word and deed in a still fallen world.

though Paul does not use the metaphor of walking as such, he reflects this language in 2 Thessalonians as well as in two companion moments of exhortation where he assumes that everything in the lives of believers is done "in the name of the Lord, Jesus."

Thus in a striking moment in his letter to the believers in Colossae, Paul concludes a considerable series of exhortations as to how to live as followers of Christ (Col. 3:12–17)—in contrast to those who live other-wise—by urging them (and indirectly those in Laodicea; 4:15–16) to do *everything*, "whether in word or deed, . . . in the name of the Lord, Jesus, giving thanks to God the Father *through* him" (3:17). This can mean only that they are to live in Colossae in such a way that the unbelievers in the city will know something about the Lord by watching his followers in action. Thus what identifies them as God's new people is also the context in which they are to live out that identification in its entirety. In a companion passage in Ephesians, believers are urged especially in the context of worship to offer their thanksgiving to God "in the name of our Lord, Jesus Christ" (Eph. 5:20).

The final group of passages in which this idiom occurs is especially, and directly, tied to what Yahweh had commanded Israel to do: take their oaths in Yahweh's name alone (Deut. 6:13). Thus in a variety of ways and circumstances Paul reflects this usage of the name as the name that (Yahweh = Lord) has now been bestowed on Christ. The phenomenon occurs first in Paul's earliest letter, where he charges the Thessalonian believers "before the Lord to have this letter read to all the brothers and sisters" (1 Thess. 5:27). When similar language is picked up again in his next letter to them, he commands them "in *the name* of the Lord, Jesus Christ," to avoid the disruptive idle (2 Thess. 3:6). This same command is enclosed a bit later (v. 12), where it is now given "in the Lord" directly to the disruptive idle. In his first letter to the believers in Corinth, Paul likewise commands and passes judgment "in the name of the Lord" (1 Cor. 1:10).

Conclusion

In every instance examined in this chapter where Paul uses the Old Testament phrase "the name of the Lord," the divine name Yahweh

(= Lord) is now the name bestowed on Christ at his exaltation. Thus all of these passages reflect various ways whereby the divine name that belonged to God alone in ancient Israel has been transferred to the one to whom that name has been given in its Greek form, *Kyrios*. In light of this reality, we turn in the next chapter to examine a whole variety of phenomena wherein Paul understands the Lord, Jesus, to have assumed roles that in the Apostle's Jewish heritage were the unique prerogatives of Yahweh alone.

9

Paul's Understanding of the Role of Jesus as Lord

Building on the evidence from the preceding chapter, in this chapter we bring together a number of affirmations, both intentional and incidental, in which Paul speaks of Jesus as Lord in a variety of roles that in the Old Testament were the unique province of Israel's God, Yahweh. Our concern is to examine how Paul perceives the risen Christ to *function* as the eternal, exalted Lord in every kind of matter on earth and in heaven.

As we have seen repeatedly throughout this study, so here Paul is presupposing rather than arguing for an understanding of Christ as acting on behalf of the Godhead. In the majority of cases these affirmations exist as something Paul argues from rather than for, since they frequently serve as the basis for what Paul will urge on these various communities of believers in their own settings, most often regarding some matter of Christian behavior.

The Eschatological Judge

We begin with a group of affirmations related to an aspect of Christ the Lord as the coming one, where he is assumed to be the end-time agent of divine justice, including both final salvation and judgment. Several moments in Paul's letters fit this category, many of them reflecting off-handed echoes of the Septuagint. Together they make it plain that the role of judge consistently assigned to Yahweh in Israel's worldview has now been assumed altogether by Christ as the *Kyrios* (= Yahweh). First we examine several instances where Paul uses the basic designation for the eschatological event, "the Day of the Lord"—passages listed in their assumed chronological order over about a ten-year span.

The Day of the Lord

1 THESSALONIANS 5:2
For you know very well that the day of the Lord will come like a thief in the night.

2 THESSALONIANS 2:1–2
We ask you, brothers and sisters, not to become easily unsettled or alarmed by the teaching . . . that the day of the Lord has already come.

1 CORINTHIANS 1:8
He will also keep you firm to the end, so that you will be blameless on the day of our Lord, Jesus Christ.

1 CORINTHIANS 5:5
Hand this man over to Satan . . . so that his spirit may be saved on the day of the Lord.

PHILIPPIANS 1:6, 9–10
He who began a good work in you will carry it on to completion until the day of Christ Jesus. . . . And this is my prayer: . . . that you . . . may be pure and blameless for the day of Christ.

One of the ways the prophets spoke of the eschatological future for God's people was with the phrase "the day of the LORD," a "day" that included both divine salvation and judgment. Indeed, in this tradition a coming day that had once held promise for a bright future was often portrayed first as a day of impending doom. Thus in one of the earlier prophetic oracles, Amos asks Israel, "Will not the day of the LORD be darkness, not light—pitch-dark, without a ray of brightness?" (Amos 5:20; cf. Isa. 2:6–22; Joel 1:15; 2:1–11).

In the early Christian community, the exaltation of the risen Christ carried with it an eager expectation of his return, the *parousia* (lit. "appearing") of Christ in glory. And it was to his anticipated coming that the community attached this biblical terminology of the "day." The language itself appears six times in Paul's letters, all with reference to Christ's second coming. In three of these moments Paul uses the precise language of the prophets, "the day of the Lord"; in another, "the Lord" is further identified as "Jesus Christ"; and in the two later passages the phrase is simply "the day of Christ [Jesus]." This is a certain instance where Paul appropriates language that had belonged exclusively to Yahweh and applies it to the expected eschatological return of the risen Lord, Jesus Christ. The Apostle again expresses this affirmation as a reality assumed to be held in common with his readers. As before, this language transfer is the result of Christ's having "the name" bestowed on him, so that the day of Yahweh is now the day of the return of the Lord, Jesus Christ, expressed frequently in terms of his appearing or coming again.

The primary reason for this shift of language was not intentionally christological. Rather, it was simply the logical outcome of the church's expectation that Christ the Lord, who had ascended and thus had assumed the ultimate place of authority at God's "right hand," is going to return again in power and glory. The *parousia* of the Lord would therefore be the chief event in the new understanding of the day of the Lord, and as in the Old Testament this *parousia* would be an event of both salvation and judgment. For Paul everything about this appearing, or coming, expressed previously as the exclusive prerogative of God, is now focused on Christ as the Lord (= Yahweh) of the Septuagint texts. We turn now to an examination of passages where Paul describes the *parousia* of the Lord.

The Parousia *of the Lord*

1 Thessalonians 3:13

May [God the Father] strengthen your hearts so that you will be blameless and holy in the presence of our God and Father when our *Lord*, Jesus, *comes with all his holy ones.*

ZECHARIAH 14:5

Then the LORD my God will come, and all the holy ones with him.

1 THESSALONIANS 4:16

For *the Lord* himself will *come down* from heaven, with a *loud command*, with the voice of the archangel and with *the trumpet call* of God.

PSALM 47:5

God has *ascended* amid *shouts of joy, the* LORD amid the sounding of *trumpets.*

In keeping with one of the predominant concerns in both of his letters to the believers in Thessalonica—the earliest letters in the Pauline corpus—Paul concludes an early prayer for them by expressing concern for their need to be blameless before God the Father at the *parousia* of the Lord (1 Thess. 3:11–13). He describes this coming with language taken directly from the prophet Zechariah (Zech. 14:5): the coming, or appearing, of *"our Lord,"* who is now identified as "Jesus," will be accompanied by "all his holy ones." Some have suggested that *hoi hagioi* ("the holy ones") in this case refers to Christian "saints" who will accompany Jesus (based on 1 Thess. 4:14), but this reading not only imports foreign matter into this text (the word *hagioi* does not appear in 1 Thess. 4) but also misses the christological import of the Zechariah text for the Apostle. As Paul will spell it out in greater detail in his follow-up letter to this same community of believers (2 Thess. 1:7), the "holy ones" in this context refers to angels, not humans. The christological import of Paul's weaving together of language from the prophets is that Zechariah refers to the *parousia* of Yahweh to the Mount of Olives when God's eschatological victory over the nations would be carried out. Thus the future coming of Yahweh, Paul implies, is now to be understood in terms of the future *parousia* of the present reigning Christ, who for the Apostle is singularly and always "the Lord."

In an equally striking instance of intertextuality in this same letter, Paul borrows language from the "ascent" of Yahweh in one of the enthronement psalms and applies it to the "descent" of Christ: "The Lord himself will *come down* from heaven," accompanied "with a loud command, with the voice of the archangel and with *the trumpet call* of God."

The italicized words in this case are a direct echo of language from the Psalter (Ps. 47:5). Again, with this bold stroke Paul applies to the risen *Lord* (= Jesus) language from the Psalter that refers to Yahweh. To be sure, Christ is not to be identified with Yahweh as such; rather, Paul understands Christ as the exalted Lord to assume the *role* that in the Old Testament was uniquely that of Israel's God, Yahweh (i.e., the LORD).

2 THESSALONIANS 1:7–8

This will happen when the Lord, Jesus, is revealed from heaven in blazing fire with his powerful angels. He will punish those who do not know God and do not obey the gospel of our Lord, Jesus.

ISAIAH 66:15

See, the LORD [Yahweh] is coming with fire, and his chariots are like a whirlwind; he will bring down his anger with fury, and his rebuke with flames of fire.

JEREMIAH 9:13 (CF. 32:23)

The LORD [Yahweh] said, ". . . they have not obeyed me, or followed my law."

In another remarkable moment of borrowed language, Paul uses the opening thanksgiving in his second letter to the Thessalonian believers as a way to encourage those who are suffering among them. In so doing he reassures them that at Christ's coming not only will they be "glorified" (2 Thess. 1:12) but their present enemies will be duly brought to justice. In the case of the Thessalonian believers, their suffering was very likely related to their acknowledgment of the risen Jesus as *Kyrios* (Lord) in the context of a free city with deep loyalties to the Roman emperor as *Kyrios*. This would explain why the Apostle would at this point highlight the role that their heavenly *Kyrios* will play in the final judgment. Thus with a series of intertextual moments, all taken from prophetic announcements of divine judgment, Paul reassures these nascent believers that the future is theirs—and thus neither Caesar's nor pagan Thessalonica's.

We will examine a number of these intertextual moments in the next two sections, but we begin with the initial depiction of Christ's coming in the introductory clauses of this very early letter (written toward the end of the second decade of the Christian faith). With a combination of language from the concluding oracles in Isaiah—where the prophet's words of judgment and hope for Jerusalem are placed in a kind of summary fashion—Paul deliberately places the risen Lord in the role Yahweh was to play. This begins with his description of the *parousia* itself. Along with echoes of his own language from the first letter ("from heaven . . . with his powerful angels"), Paul describes the revelation of *the Lord*, Jesus, as *"in blazing fire,"* resulting in punishment on "those who do not know God *and do not obey* the gospel of our *Lord*, Jesus" (2 Thess. 1:7–8).

The italicized words in the first part of Paul's sentence are taken directly from a moment in Isaiah where the "LORD" is Yahweh (Isa. 66:15). But for Paul the Lord who will come with blazing fire to mete out justice is none other than "our Lord, Jesus." Similarly, his description of the Lord punishing those who "do not obey the gospel of our Lord, Jesus," seems to echo a poignant moment in Jeremiah where some present judgments of Yahweh against Israel are expressed in terms of their not having "obeyed [Yahweh] or followed [his] law" (Jer. 9:13). In Paul's case, however, this language is applied to outsiders—namely, people who "do not obey the gospel of our Lord, Jesus." As before, Paul's identification of the risen Lord is not as Yahweh per se. Rather, by his having had "the name" (*Kyrios* = Yahweh) bestowed on him, the risen Christ will assume Yahweh's divine roles when he comes as judge. Picking up on this usage, we now turn to an examination of further passages where Paul clearly understands that the Lord, Jesus, will assume the role of judge for his own people as well as his enemies.

The Present and Eschatological Judge of His People

One of the more noteworthy instances where Paul describes Jesus as sharing in divine prerogatives is when Paul describes Jesus as the "Lord" who assumes Yahweh's divine role as the one who serves as judge of both his own people and the whole world. We begin by examining passages where Paul describes Christ judging his own people. Such passages occur several times in Paul's earlier letters, and in every instance he is echoing passages from the Septuagint that refer to *Kyrios* (= Yahweh), which Paul then applies to Christ as the risen Lord.

1 Thessalonians 4:6

The Lord will punish all those who commit such sins, as we told you and warned you before.

Psalm 94:1

The Lord [Yahweh] is a God who avenges. O God who avenges, shine forth.

In his warning to the Thessalonian believers (1 Thess. 4:6), Paul's wording is just unusual enough to suggest that he is echoing language from the opening words of Psalm 94, where the Lord (= Yahweh) is identified as "a God who avenges" (v. 1). Although contemporary English versions do not use similar verbs in these two cases, Paul's Greek word, which is used adjectivally (lit. "the avenger Lord"), seems very likely to be an echo of the language with which this Psalm begins, as suggested in the Greek text.[1] In a context where a brother has abused another brother in a matter of sexual immorality, Paul assures the offender that "the Lord [Christ] is an avenger in all these things" (1 Thess. 4:6 NRSV). Here is a case where Paul seems very easily to have transferred to Christ (as "Lord") biblical language that belongs to Yahweh alone.

1 Corinthians 4:4–5

It is the Lord who judges me. Therefore judge nothing before the appointed time; wait until the Lord comes. He will bring to *light* what is *hidden in darkness* and will expose the motives of the heart. At that time each will receive their praise from God.

Daniel 2:22

[God] reveals deep and *hidden* things; he knows what lies *in darkness*, and *light* dwells with him.

---

1. Paul's word, *ekdikos*, is difficult to render in English. The *Greek-English Lexicon of the New Testament and Other Early Christian Literature*, 3rd ed., ed. Frederick William Danker (Chicago: University of Chicago Press, 1979), 301, defines it as "pertaining to justice being done so as to rectify wrong done to another." The English word "avenge" is defined in the standard English dictionary (*Merriam-Webster's Collegiate Dictionary*, 11th ed. [Springfield, MA: Merriam-Webster, 2014], 85) as "to take vengeance for" or "to exact satisfaction for." It would thus seem to any ordinary reader that *ekdikos* and "avenger" are not quite interchangeable! This is one of those rare instances where probably the richest language in history falls just a bit short. It simply does not work well—correct as it might have been in the English of another day—to say, "The Lord will rectify such people's wrongdoing"!

Toward the end of the first major issue he takes up with the believers in Corinth (1 Cor. 1:10–4:21), after taking exception to some of them sitting in judgment of him, Paul makes it plain that the only one with the right to judge him is "the Lord," whose servant he is (1 Cor. 4:4). Thus even though he knows of nothing that would be the cause for such judgment on their part, he goes on to acknowledge that this in itself does not mean final justification for him since ultimately the Lord judges, or examines,[2] him, which here clearly indicates the eschatological judgment to come.

In this instance, as in others, the Apostle concludes by including the Corinthians themselves in this final examination by the Lord. So they must be careful not to judge anything "before the appointed time," when the Lord (Christ) himself comes and (literally) "will bring to light the hidden things of darkness and will lay bare the plans of people's hearts" (1 Cor. 4:5, my trans.). In this apparent echoing of language from Daniel (whether intended to be so or not), Paul reminds the Corinthians that at the time when Christ will exercise his judgment of "light," the role of God the Father will be to "praise" those found worthy by the Lord's judgment (v. 5). This combination makes it quite clear that Paul understands the final judgment of believers to be a uniquely divine prerogative—now assumed to be that of the risen Lord, Jesus Christ.

2 CORINTHIANS 5:9–11

So we make it our goal to please [the Lord], whether we are at home in the body or away from it. For we must all appear before the judgment seat of Christ, so that each of us may receive what is due us for the things done while in the body, whether good or bad. Since, then, we know what it is to fear the Lord, we try to persuade others.

Along with the preceding moments where Paul echoes the language of the Old Testament in the matter of Christ the Lord serving as judge at the end times, in his second letter to the Corinthian believers Paul describes Christ as Lord assuming the prerogative of God as judge at

---

2. This is another instance where various translators have tended toward quite different words to render Paul's Greek verb (*anakrinō*) into English.

the final assize (2 Cor. 5:9–11), though he does so in this case without using language from any specific moment in the Septuagint. Toward the end of a considerable narrative and appeal, concluding his reflection on the future of the present body that is destined to decay but then to be once again "clothed" in the eschaton (vv. 2–4), Paul uses himself as an example that serves as a couched appeal to the Corinthians. He does this in three ways.

First, Paul expresses his desire to live so as "to please" the Lord (2 Cor. 5:9), an Old Testament idea that in Paul is expressed ordinarily in terms of pleasing "God" (e.g., 1 Thess. 4:1; 2 Cor. 5:9; Rom. 8:8). But here, as in his earlier letter to these believers (1 Cor. 7:32), "the Lord," Christ, is the one he seeks to please.

Second, the reason for this is that "we must all appear before the judgment seat [bēma] of Christ" (2 Cor. 5:10). The word bēma refers to the chair that would be placed on a structure of some sort above the people in the Greek agora (public market), where a magistrate would sit and listen to accusations or complaints and then mete out various kinds of judgments. In this remarkable sentence Paul asserts that Christ the Lord will assume God's role in issuing final judgment on his own people, "so that each of us may receive what is due us for the things done while in the body, whether good or bad" (v. 10).

Here is a case where Paul places Christ, the risen Lord, in the role that everyone in his native Jewish community considered to be the absolute prerogative of God alone. One thing that was certain in Jewish understanding was Yahweh's own justice and role as the absolute ruler of the universe. This in turn meant that Yahweh, and Yahweh alone, would mete out eschatological judgment on all people at the end. So here again, without argument or an attempt to make a christological statement per se, Paul offhandedly attributes such judgment to Christ, the Lord whom he strives to please for that very reason.

Third, the ultimate appeal for the Corinthian believers to follow the Apostle's own example comes at the end of the passage, where Paul speaks of (literally) "knowing therefore the fear of the Lord" (v. 11, my trans.). This is a clear case where a distinctive Old Testament phrase regarding Yahweh is applied directly (here only, as it turns out) to Christ, the exalted Lord before whom both Paul and the Corinthians must appear at the end.[3]

What is perhaps most striking about all of these various moments in Paul's letters is how easily and apparently unselfconsciously he attributes to the risen Lord what are absolute prerogatives of Yahweh, the God of Israel. Indeed, this feature makes a singular moment in Paul's letter to the believers in Rome difficult for interpreters to handle since in that case he writes, "For we will all stand before God's judgment seat," where "each of us will give an account of ourselves to God" (Rom. 14:10, 12). But in this case, the very fact that scholars have regularly found this issue so difficult to resolve is precisely because Paul can so easily make this kind of interchange between the exalted Lord and God the Father. Here, then, is what appears to be certain evidence that Christ's full equality with God the Father is something Paul simply takes for granted and expresses in these various ways as a matter of course. Significantly, he does all of this without trying to place Christ and the Father on equal ground. By the time these letters had been written, such an interchange had for him now become something normal. Paul has simply presupposed this high Christology as a reality held equally by himself and his readers—and this within two decades of the cross and resurrection.

The Eschatological Judge of the Wicked

Perhaps one of the most telling moments in which Paul describes Christ assuming the various roles that belong exclusively to Yahweh in the Old Testament is when Paul describes Christ with the ultimate divine prerogative of executing judgment (= justice) on the wicked. It is one thing for the believers' Lord to be judge in matters pertaining to *them*. But from Paul's perspective, Christ the Lord is also the final judge of those who have rejected him, many of whom have caused grief for the Lord's people. Here Paul is especially matter-of-fact in attributing to Jesus the prerogatives of Yahweh, as he does twice in one of his

---

3. This is also yet another instance where one of the world's richest languages fails to have an adequate adjective since "fear" in English is consistently a negative idea. Paul's clear point is rather that true believers live in constant reverential awe in the presence of their Lord—as in "the fear of the LORD is the beginning of knowledge" (Prov. 1:7).

earliest letters, 2 Thessalonians, written a little less than two decades after Christ's death and resurrection.

2 THESSALONIANS 1:9–10

They will be punished with everlasting destruction and shut out from the presence of the Lord and from the glory of his might on the day he comes to be glorified in his holy people and to be marveled at among all those who have believed.

PSALM 68:35

You, God, are awesome in your sanctuary.

PSALM 89:7

In the council of his holy ones God is greatly feared; he is more awesome than all who surround him.

ISAIAH 2:10

Go into the rocks, hide in the ground from the fearful presence of the LORD and the splendor of his majesty!

After a description of Christ's coming as eschatological judge that echoes language from Isaiah 66 (2 Thess. 1:7–8), Paul turns next to focus on the judgment of the wicked he has just mentioned. Paul declares that these people "will be punished with everlasting destruction and shut out *from the presence of the Lord and from the glory of his might*" (v. 9). The apparent awkwardness of this clause results from the fact that the italicized words are taken directly from the Septuagint's rendering of Isaiah 2:10, a "day of the Lord" oracle of judgment against Judah. Just as in the Isaiah passage, the result of God's judgment means to be cut off from the divine presence (the face of the Lord), who is now assumed to be the risen Lord, Christ Jesus. Paul's attribution of the Isaianic oracle to Christ is made the more remarkable by the (in this case seemingly unnecessary) inclusion of the final phrase, "from the glory of his might." Here again, Paul adapts language from Isaiah that refers to Yahweh and appropriates it in his description of Christ's judgment on the Thessalonians' present enemies.

Paul's characteristically long sentence concludes on a note about the Lord's own people when the wicked are being judged. Again the Apostle appears to be reflecting the Septuagint for this description, this time echoing a passage in the Psalter where the referent is *Elohim* (God) rather than Yahweh ("the LORD"). Nonetheless, in Paul's sentence "the Lord" is still the subject of the verb "comes" (2 Thess. 1:10). Thus, using language from two moments in the Psalter (Ps. 68:35; 89:7), Paul contrasts the preceding judgment of their enemies with the greater reality that Christ the Lord will be "glorified in his holy people [saints]" and "marveled at among all who have believed" (2 Thess. 1:10). Thus this entire long sentence (vv. 6–10) is one of the more significant moments in Paul's letters where several Old Testament *Kyrios* moments are all attributed to the Lord, Christ. For Paul, it is now Christ the risen Lord who is the coming one; it is Christ the risen Lord who assumes the role of divine judge of the wicked; and it is Christ the risen Lord who will be glorified in his people at his coming. So even though Paul stops short of calling Christ either Yahweh or *Theos* (God)—which in Pauline usage is always a referent not to the Son but to the Father of the Son, and thus to those who belong to the Son—his intertextual use of the Septuagint's *Kyrios* (= *Adonai*/Yahweh) allows Paul to predicate his conviction of Christ's full deity.

2 THESSALONIANS 2:8

And then the lawless one will be revealed, whom the Lord, Jesus, will overthrow with the breath of his mouth and destroy by the splendor of his coming.

ISAIAH 11:4

He will strike the earth with the rod of his mouth; with the breath of his lips he will slay the wicked.

Finally, in 2 Thessalonians 2:8 Paul again places Christ, the risen Lord, in the role of eschatological judge, but this is the only time Paul describes Christ fulfilling an actual messianic passage from the prophetic tradition. In keeping with the expected Messiah's role of meting out God's justice on earth when he comes, Paul uses a combined form of the language of the prophet Isaiah (Isa. 11:4). Here the prophet's line "with the rod of his mouth; with the breath of his lips he will slay the wicked" is condensed into Paul's phrase "will overthrow with the breath of his mouth." But the Apostle does so by putting this into the eschatological future, when "the Lord, Jesus, will overthrow [the wicked] with the breath of his mouth," to which Paul adds, "and destroy [them] by the splendor of his coming." Here Paul has it both ways. The exalted Lord is also the Messiah, but now the crucified one as the risen Lord fulfills the role of Isaiah's messianic figure in executing God's (now final) judgment against the wicked. And what is once again so striking is the absolute ease with which Paul does this in one of his earliest letters.

Jesus the Lord: Invoked in Prayer

In chapter 1 we noted that Paul's Christ devotion included both worship and prayer directed toward Christ as deity. We now spell out in more detail the christological implications that lie behind the several passages noted there. Indeed, nowhere in the Pauline corpus is Paul's understanding of the Son's "equality with God" (Phil. 2:6) more telling than in his prayers offered to the risen Lord as one would ordinarily offer them to God alone. Here we note the various ways this happens, concentrating on the reality that such prayer is in every case addressed to the "Lord," who received *that* "name" at his exaltation and vindication.

Prayer to "the Lord" in the Thessalonian Correspondence

1 Thessalonians 3:11–13

Now may our God and Father himself and our Lord, Jesus, clear the way for us to come to you. May the Lord make your love increase and overflow for each other and for everyone else, just as ours does for you. May he strengthen your hearts so that you will be blameless and holy in the presence of our God and Father when our Lord, Jesus, comes with all his holy ones.

2 Thessalonians 2:16–17

May our Lord, Jesus Christ himself, and God our Father, who loved us and by his grace gave us eternal encouragement and good hope, encourage your hearts and strengthen you in every good deed and word.

2 Thessalonians 3:5

May the Lord direct your hearts into God's love and Christ's perseverance.

2 Thessalonians 3:16

Now may the Lord of peace himself give you peace at all times and in every way. The Lord be with all of you.

On four occasions in Paul's two earliest letters to his churches, most likely written toward the end of the second decade of the Christian faith (ca. 49–50 CE), Paul reports to the believers in Thessalonica how he is praying for them. In each case he uses the optative mood—what grammarians in such cases refer to as a "prayer-wish," meaning simply a form of indirection—to express prayer to God with the recipients in view and for their sake. The most remarkable thing about these four prayers is how the deity is addressed in each case.

In the first instance (1 Thess. 3:11), God the Father is mentioned first and intensified by means of the reflexive pronoun "himself," with "our Lord, Jesus," in the second position. Significantly, this in turn is followed by a verb not in the plural but in the singular, indicating that both are being addressed together as one. This otherwise grammatical "glitch" is then followed (vv. 12–13) by additional petitions addressed to *the Lord alone*, asking him for divine favors that only God could bestow: that their love increase and abound for one another and for all with the goal that their hearts be strengthened in holiness so that they will be blameless before God the Father at Christ's coming. The remainder of Paul's prayer thus reinforces the natural implications of the two divine persons being addressed with a verb in the singular. As a teacher in an earlier day aptly put it, "Let me listen to you pray, and I will write your theology."

In the second prayer (2 Thess. 2:16–17), the pattern from the first prayer is reversed. The prayer is still addressed to both Father and Son, but it begins in this case as prayer addressed to "the Lord, Jesus Christ," while the elaboration that follows has to do with the Father. Nonetheless, the two actual verbs that form the content of the prayer are used elsewhere in these letters with regard to the work of both the Father ("encourage your hearts") and of the Son ("strengthen you"). So the prayer in each case seems intentionally addressed to both God the Father and the Lord, Jesus.

More remarkable still are the two final prayers, which are both addressed to "the Lord" alone (2 Thess. 3:5, 16). The first instance appears to be a deliberate echo of the prayer in his first letter to these relatively new believers (1 Thess. 3:11), in this case as a parting prayer for them. Now using language from one of the prayers of David recorded in 1 Chronicles 29:18, Paul addresses the one who has been given the "name," that he, "the Lord" (= Jesus), direct the believers' hearts into God's love and Christ's patience.

In the second instance, the formal conclusion to his letter, Paul requests Christ, "the Lord of peace," to grant them his *shalom*, or "peace" in the sense of a well-arranged heart that provides restfulness before God. Everything about this remarkable moment echoes a singularly divine appellation and prerogative, now addressed to the risen Lord.

Some have argued that these latter two moments are not actually prayers directed to Christ since they only mention "the Lord." However, as we have seen repeatedly, Paul consistently uses *Kyrios* as a referent to Christ alone, and not once to God the Father. Paul's own identification markers should thus dictate our understanding of the word in moments like these. This is especially so in the present case, since in his correspondence with the Thessalonian believers Paul himself consistently identifies Christ as *Kyrios*. And in this passage in particular, he is repeating the identification from the immediately preceding prayer (2 Thess. 2:16–17).

Thus, in his letter to believers in Thessalonica, Paul consistently addresses prayer to the present reigning Lord, Jesus Christ—a prerogative the Jewish community reserved for God alone. That he does this in such a straightforward way, apparently assuming his readers will take no notice of it, suggests that this had long been a part of his life of devotion, which he has shared in common with his churches. Rather than presenting something novel to these believers, Paul simply reminds them of what they have already been taught and urges them to live accordingly.

Other Prayers Addressed to "the Lord"

2 CORINTHIANS 13:14

May the grace of the Lord, Jesus Christ, and the love of God, and the fellowship of the Holy Spirit be with you all.

1 CORINTHIANS 16:22

Come, Lord [*Marana tha*].

2 Corinthians 12:8–9

Three times I pleaded with the Lord to take it away from me. But he said to me, "My grace is sufficient for you, for my power is made perfect in weakness."

The prayer reports like those Paul mentions in the Thessalonian correspondence do not occur elsewhere in the rest of the corpus, except for the benedictory "grace" that concludes all the letters addressed to churches, including Philemon. This happens most often in the following form: "May the grace of our Lord, Jesus Christ, be with you." It takes an altogether different form in Ephesians and lacks the phrase "of our Lord, Jesus Christ" in Colossians. But in each of these instances, there are two reasons to believe that this is a form of prayer addressed to Jesus as Lord.

First, if we replaced "the Lord" with any other divine title or name, it would be clear that this is indeed a form of prayer. It would work perfectly as a prayer, for example, if we substituted "God our Father" for "our Lord" so that it read, "May the grace of God our Father be with you." If this were the case, it would be universally recognized as prayer. But, interestingly, Paul never does that; he always expresses his benediction in some form of "the grace of our Lord, Jesus Christ, be with you." Clearly such an expression would not work if we substituted a nondivine being for "our Lord." So, for example, no one would even think of saying, "May the grace of the great archangel Michael be with you." More unthinkable yet would be such a benediction in the name of a mere human, even a divinely exalted one. Thus this usage is a form of prayer report, pure and simple, and it is therefore another example of Paul's presuppositional high Christology. No Jew of the first century could imagine addressing prayer to one who is merely human and not also truly divine. And despite Paul's Damascus road "conversion," the Apostle not only retained his Jewishness as such but also at times made a considerable point of it.

Second, that these passages are intended as benedictory *prayers* is confirmed by the singular triadic elaboration found at the conclusion of Paul's second letter to the believers in Corinth (2 Cor. 13:14). Here Paul begins with the standard line, "May the grace of our Lord, Jesus Christ," but then for reasons that are not at all clear he adds, "and the love of God, and fellowship [*koinonia*] of the Holy Spirit." Scholars agree that this triadic benediction is a form of prayer, but surely Paul's benedictions are no less so when Paul's phrase, "the grace of our Lord, Jesus Christ," lacks the addition of God the Father and the Holy Spirit.

The remaining instances of prayer reports also occur in the Corinthian correspondence. In the one instance (1 Cor. 16:22), we are given in its Aramaic formulation the actual content of the earliest known prayer to be used among followers of Christ: *Marana tha* ("Come, Lord"). By any definition, this is clearly a prayer addressed to Christ as Lord.

The next instance occurs in his second letter to these same believers (2 Cor. 12:8–9) and has a unique, twofold feature: (1) it is addressed to "the Lord" for a very personal matter of which (2) Paul reports the answer, which was not what he prayed for. "Three times," he says, "I pleaded with the Lord to take [the thorn in my flesh] away from me." And Paul then reports the Lord's response: "My grace is sufficient for you."

To be sure, the answer Paul received was quite in keeping with what he had come to know of Christ his Lord. Paul had already learned—and had made a considerable point of the fact to these same believers in his earlier letter to them—that God's power is evident in the "weakness" of the ultimate oxymoron: a crucified Messiah (1 Cor. 1:18–25). As he had already put it there: "The foolishness of God is wiser than human wisdom, and the weakness of God is stronger than human strength" (v. 25). The present passage makes it equally clear that Paul himself was in the process of learning that discipleship meant to live a cruciform life—that is, a life that is conformed to Christ as the crucified one. Thus Christ responds: "*My* grace is sufficient" because "*my* power is made perfect in [your] weakness" (2 Cor. 12:9).

By anyone's definition this passage can be understood only as a report of Paul's prayer addressed singularly to Christ as Lord, which in this case includes the unusual feature of a response to his prayer by Christ his Lord. Such prayer with its recorded answer would seem to put considerable theological pressure on a monotheist who had not included the Lord in the divine identity, which suggests that Paul was indeed living for, and talking about, the one God in a triadic way long before such an under-standing of God needed to be spelled out in the context of the later creeds.

As we will discuss further in the concluding chapter, such a triadic understanding is expressed most certainly by Paul at the beginning of his corrections of the abuses of Spirit-giftings in his first letter to this believing community in Corinth: "There are different kinds of gifts, but the same Spirit distributes them. There are different kinds of service, but the same Lord. There are different kinds of working, but in all of them and in everyone it is the same God at work" (1 Cor. 12:4–6). This passage is the first of eight such moments in the Pauline corpus of letters that provide the basis from which a later articulation of the triune nature of the one God becomes an absolute necessity. But at this point Paul is not attempting to formulate trinitarian theology; he is simply expressing a conviction that is presupposed to be held in common between himself and the believers in Corinth. What is at stake in these passages is not theology but behavior in the context of worship, having to do with Spirit-manifestations in the gathered community.

Conclusion

In this chapter we have observed further instances of the pattern we have seen throughout Paul's letters: in his application of the roles of Yahweh to Jesus as well as in his various reports of prayers to Jesus, Paul assumes that he and his letters' recipients share the same high Christology, which he then argues from rather than having to argue for. The Apostle does not expect any of his readers, or hearers, to be shocked or startled by what he asserts. Rather, what makes the christological point so thoroughly compelling is that this startlingly high Christology is something Paul barely expects his readers to take notice of at all.

10

Jesus the Lord

Sharer of Other Divine Prerogatives

In this chapter we discuss a number of other instances throughout Paul's letters where Christ "the Lord" shares a considerable variety of prerogatives that in the Jewish worldview belong exclusively to God. We begin with several instances where the risen Lord has assumed the role of *Kyrios* ("Lord" = Yahweh) and where he is thereby seen to have assumed the divine privileges inherent in the Septuagint text.

Christ, the Lord of Septuagint Texts

Boast in the Lord

1 CORINTHIANS 1:31
Therefore, as it is written: "Let the one who boasts boast in the Lord."

JEREMIAH 9:24
"But let the one who boasts boast about this: that they have the understanding to know me, that I am the LORD [Yahweh], who exercises kindness, justice and righteousness on earth, for in these I delight," declares the LORD.

The language of boasting, either as a verb, verbal noun, or abstract noun, occurs fifty-nine times in the New Testament, fifty-five of them in Paul's letters, and thirty-nine of these in the Corinthian letters alone—which suggests that Paul considered this a significant issue in the Corinthian church! Specifically, as the first matter addressed in the first of these letters, "division" in the "household" over their nonresident teachers or leaders, especially Apollos and Paul, was based primarily on the criterion of eloquence (1 Cor. 1:10–12). Significantly, and brilliantly, Paul does not take them on directly regarding the matter of boasting itself; he will come to that a bit later (2:6–16). Rather, he focuses first on the *object* of their boast. In so doing, he uses the language of boasting in his response to them not at all negatively but rather by drawing from an important moment in the prophet Jeremiah (Jer. 9:23–24), of which Paul makes considerable use throughout an entire paragraph (1 Cor. 1:26–31).

That Paul is here intentionally making use of this passage from Jeremiah is evident from his preceding sentences (1 Cor. 1:26–28), where his categories for what people put their boast (= confidence) in are the "wise" and "influential [powerful]" and those "of noble birth"—an apparently ad hoc updating for the Corinthians' sake of Jeremiah's categories: "wisdom," "strength," and "riches" (Jer. 9:23).

Paul's argument then concludes with the clause, "as it is written," followed by a paraphrase of the Jeremiah text to address the issue at hand in Corinth: "Let the one who boasts boast in the Lord" (1 Cor. 1:31). In Jeremiah, the Septuagint's *Kyrios* glosses *Adonai* (= Yahweh), whereas for Paul the "Lord" in whom the Corinthians are to "boast" is Christ himself—a most remarkable reworking of the Jeremiah passage indeed, especially since their "boast" is now to be in the crucified one (cf. Phil. 3:3, 8, 10). Since the Septuagint is the *only* Bible these nascent believers, both Jew and Greek, would have known, there can be very little question as to where Paul was going with this somewhat gentle letdown of believers who had become altogether too high on themselves. It is now Christ the Lord, the crucified one, in whom alone they may—and indeed *must*—boast, where boasting is understood not as showing off but as putting one's full confidence in something or someone.

The Mind of the Lord

1 CORINTHIANS 2:16

"Who has known the mind of the Lord so as to instruct him?" But we have the mind of Christ.

ISAIAH 40:13

Who can fathom the Spirit of the LORD, or instruct the LORD as his counselor?

From as early as in his first letter to the Corinthian believers, Paul has been arguing vigorously with them, almost certainly to their chagrin, that God's true wisdom and power are to be found in a crucified Messiah (1 Cor. 1:18–2:5). The Apostle next feels the need to explain further (perhaps somewhat ironically to those confident of their Spirit-gifting) that the only way he and they can have this true wisdom is by revelation from the Spirit (2:6–16)—as is made abundantly clear later in the letter (chaps. 12–14). But in the present context, he concludes this part of his argument by citing Isaiah's poignant question: "Who has known the mind of the Lord so as to instruct him?" (2:16).

As in other instances, so too one might be led to read "the Lord" in this citation as referring to God the Father. But Paul offers his own interpretation, which disallows such a view. Here is yet another Old Testament Yahweh passage that is now to be understood in terms of Christ. "But we have the mind *of Christ*," he concludes, thus interchanging "the LORD" (= Yahweh) of the Septuagint with "the Lord, Christ"—once again revealing his especially high Christology.

Beloved of the Lord

2 THESSALONIANS 2:13

But we ought always to thank God for you, brothers and sisters loved by the Lord, because God chose you as firstfruits.

DEUTERONOMY 33:12

About Benjamin he said: "Let the beloved of the LORD rest secure in him."

In yet another truly remarkable moment of intertextuality, in his second thanksgiving in his second letter to the Thessalonians Paul addresses these believers as those "loved by *the Lord*." This unique moment in the entire Pauline corpus can easily go unnoticed by modern readers (so much so that it fails even to make it as a marginal notation in the current NIV, which is otherwise especially up to speed on these matters). Nonetheless, what needs to be noted is that Paul's language is precisely that of his Greek Bible, the Septuagint, from Moses's blessing of the tribe of Benjamin: "Let the beloved of the LORD [= Yahweh] rest secure in him" (Deut. 33:12).

Thus in a moment of needed reassurance, those whom Paul had earlier described as loved by God (1 Thess. 1:4)—and will do so again in a follow-up moment (2 Thess. 2:16)—are here addressed in the language of Paul's own Benjaminite family crest (see Phil. 3:5): beloved of the Lord. Even if the Thessalonians may not themselves have caught the reference, Paul is once again referring to Christ as their Lord, as he makes the interchange between God and Christ throughout this letter.

The Lord Be with You

2 THESSALONIANS 3:16
The Lord be with all of you.

RUTH 2:4
Boaz . . . greeted the harvesters, "The LORD [Yahweh] be with you!"

In one final, equally remarkable moment of intertextuality in the Thessalonian correspondence, Paul signs off his second letter to them with what appears to be an echo of the personal greeting that thrived among Yahwists in ancient Israel, "The LORD be with you." In this case it is an echo from one of Paul's Benjaminite predecessors (see Rom. 11:1). In the book of Ruth, we are told that Boaz greeted his workers, "The LORD be with you" (2:4; cf. the angelic greetings in Judg. 6:12 and Luke 1:28). This is another instance where Paul's *Kyrios* (= *Adonai*/Yahweh) is applied to Christ—verified in this case not only by the surrounding matter but also by (a) the twofold identification of Christ as "Lord" in this letter in conjunction with *Theos* as Father (2 Thess. 1:2; 2:16) and (b) Paul's consistent use of *Kyrios* to refer to Christ throughout his corpus.

Paul thus concludes his letter with this historic greeting as a prayer-wish that the exalted Lord would continue to be present with the believers in Thessalonica as Christ in his incarnation was with us when he came among us in our likeness in order to redeem. And, as we will discuss in the concluding chapter, Christ would be with them by the Spirit, who is at one and the same time known by Paul as the Spirit of God and the Spirit of Christ, as is made certain by his usage in his letter to the believers in Rome (Rom. 8:9–11).

The Lord Is Near

PHILIPPIANS 4:5

The Lord is near.

PSALM 145:18

The Lord is near to all who call on him.

In one of the more puzzling affirmations in his letters, Paul picks up David's precise language from the Psalter as a means to encourage the believers in Philippi. The puzzle is twofold: first, whether it is a word about the present or an affirmation about the future, and, second, whether it goes with what precedes or follows. That is, does the Apostle intend, "Let your gentleness be evident to all [because] the Lord is near," or, more likely in my view, "The Lord is near, [so] do not be anxious about anything" (Phil. 4:5–6)? In either case, this is yet another instance where Paul has adopted language about Yahweh from the Septuagint and applied it to Christ. The Apostle so lived and breathed the language of his Bible, as is evident everywhere in his letters, that he sometimes finds himself speaking in such an unusual manner as we find here!

Kyrios and *Theos* Share Prerogatives

In several instances in his letters, Paul interchanges a variety of divine attributes or activities between God (*Theos*) and the Lord (*Kyrios*). To be sure, not all of these are strictly *divine* prerogatives, but what is striking in each case is how easily and seemingly without deliberation Paul can make these interchanges. Rather than group or prioritize these passages, we simply list them below in their assumed chronological order. We deliberately limit our discussion to the first four letters in Paul's corpus (1 and 2 Thessalonians and 1 and 2 Corinthians) since most everything after those letters would be repetition.

Christian Existence as Being in Christ/God

1 THESSALONIANS 1:1

To the church of the Thessalonians in God the Father and the Lord, Jesus Christ: Grace and peace to you.

The first mention of God and Christ together in the Pauline corpus appears in the very first line in Paul's very first letter (1 Thess. 1:1; cf. 2 Thess. 1:1)—in this case as the double (grammatical) objects of a single prepositional phrase ("in God the Father and the Lord, Jesus Christ"). It is a phrase unlike any in Paul's other letters. Here he designates the church of the Thessalonians as equally and simultaneously existing *in God the Father and the Lord, Jesus Christ*. In later letters he will frequently speak of believers as being "in Christ," but here he speaks of them as also being "in God."

The christological significance of this phrase is considerable indeed. For here is a significant twofold affirmation. First, God and Christ are together understood as the sphere in which believers exist; that is, they are simultaneously in God and in the Lord. And thus, second, to exist *in God* means at the same time to exist *in Christ*. It is not as though these believers lived in a twofold sphere of existence. Rather, for the Apostle to be "in Christ" means to be "in God" and vice versa—hence the reason Paul can later place them "in Christ" alone, because they are for him thereby automatically "in God" as well. Here, as the first thing the believers in Thessalonica will hear, is the affirmation that they exist simultaneously in both the Father and the Son.

How the Thessalonians might have heard this one can only guess, but we can be certain of what Paul intended by it because of the way he extrapolates these two realities in his later letter to the believers in Galatia (Gal. 4:4–7). Having made us "sons," the same God who "sent his

Son" likewise sent "the Spirit of his Son into our hearts." We are thus able to use the Son's own language and call God "Father," whom we now address in Jesus's native tongue, "*Abba*," a diminutive that in English would mean something close to "dear Father."[1] What is striking indeed is the intimate familial ring of this language—and this from a Jewish man who grew up in a community that would never even mention the name of Yahweh, substituting "Lord" in its place for fear of speaking the name in vain!

The Grace of the Lord/God

The wish of "grace" for Paul's churches is another place in his letters where the divine prerogatives are equally shared between God and Christ (the Lord), but in this case in an interesting variety of combinations. On the one hand, Paul's letters almost all *begin* with the doublet "grace to you and peace," and always in this order since the second flows out of the first.[2] The source of this grace is invariably identified in turn: "from [both] God the Father and the Lord, Jesus Christ." Paul's own consistent usage—quite decisively it would seem, suggesting that he intends for his audience to hear it in this sequence—begins with "grace to you," based on Christ's redemptive love on the believers' behalf, and concludes with the proper follow-up, "and peace." Thus God's initiating action on our behalf should result in "peace," or what someone once described as a well-arranged heart.

On the other hand, most of the letters *sign off* with the singular benedictory prayer, "May the grace of the Lord [= Christ Jesus] be with you," beginning with his first letter to the Thessalonians (1 Thess. 5:28). Yet in the body of Paul's letters grace is far more often expressed as coming from God the Father, with three notable exceptions where it is an attribute of Christ the Lord (2 Cor. 8:9; 12:9; 1 Tim. 1:14). This kind of interchange is not the result of a well thought-out theology but has

---

1. Indeed, our closest English equivalent would be "Daddy," but in English that carries too many other connotations that would not be true of "*Abba*" for us ever to so render it. This is a clear example where a diminutive in one language is simply not transferable to its equivalent in another language and is therefore not truly translatable.

2. This is also why it is not quite precise when rendered (consistently in the English versions), "grace and peace to you."

become, by this point, simply a matter-of-fact kind of usage between Paul and his churches.

The Peace of the Lord/God—the Lord/God of Peace

The same interchangeability between *Theos* and *Kyrios* regarding "grace" is also true of its companion "peace," which appears together with "grace" in all the salutations, and, as noted above, is always presented in the order "grace to you, and peace." Elsewhere in the body of the letters there is again an interesting expression of interchangeability. On the one hand, the phrase "the peace of God" occurs only once in the corpus (Phil. 4:7), as does its counterpart, "the peace of the Lord" (2 Thess. 3:16). On the other hand, the descriptor, "the God of peace," occurs six times. It occurs four times alone (1 Thess. 5:23; Rom. 15:33; 16:20; Phil. 4:9)—a form that is actually quite rare in the Old Testament. It further occurs once in the compound "God of love and peace" (2 Cor. 13:11), and is implied once in a contrast with "disorder" (1 Cor. 14:33).

In its second occurrence in the Thessalonian correspondence, Paul prays that "the Lord of peace" will "himself give you peace at all times" (2 Thess. 3:16). This line should be read as a prayer, and in this case it is a prayer offered to Christ alone—a striking feature that often goes unnoticed because of the casual, presuppositional way such interchange of language comes to us, which has also now become so commonplace.

Walk Worthy of the Lord/God

Another of these off-the-cuff, unintentional interchanges between "Lord" and "God" occurs in Paul's appropriation of the Old Testament concept of "walking." In the New Testament this is a consistent metaphor, taken over from the Old Testament, having to do with how a person lives before God and in the world. In his first letter to the believers in Thessalonica, the Apostle implores these new believers to walk worthy of *the God* who called them, even in the midst of present difficulties (1 Thess. 2:12). In a similar moment in a much later letter—this time by way of a prayer-report—he urges that the believers walk "worthy of the Lord," which in context can refer only to Christ, so as to "please him in every way" (Col. 1:10).

As elsewhere this is an interchange that most later readers would scarcely notice, since either Christ or God fits well within one's expectations when reading Paul's letters. And that is precisely our reason for calling the reader's attention to it here. This is illustrative of an assumed Christology of the highest order without intent on the Apostle's part and yet expected by him to be shared by his readers or hearers.

The Divine Presence at the Parousia

Closely associated with Israel's understanding of the divine *glory* in the Old Testament is the concept of God's *presence*, as the interchange between these two ideas regarding the tabernacle and temple makes clear. Picking up the latter theme, Paul can speak interchangeably of being in the presence of the Lord or of God, depending on his point of emphasis at a given moment. Thus in his first mention of Christ's *parousia* ("coming"), which appears in his earliest letter, Paul speaks of the Thessalonian believers as "our joy, . . . the crown in which we will glory" when together they will appear "in the presence of *our Lord, Jesus,* when he comes" (1 Thess. 2:19). A few sentences later, at the conclusion of his prayer (3:11–13), he speaks of being (literally) "in the presence of *our God and Father* at the *parousia* of our Lord, Jesus" (v. 13, my trans.). This is yet another instance of the interchange between "God" and "the Lord"—and these are the words of an ardent monotheist!

The Lord/God Who Strengthens Believers

In the same prayer just noted above, Paul continues by expressing his desire that "the *Lord* [= Christ] . . . strengthen your hearts so that you will be blameless and holy" (1 Thess. 3:12–13). Similarly, in his second letter to his friends in Thessalonica, he assures them that "the *Lord* . . . will strengthen you and protect you from the evil one" (2 Thess. 3:3). In between these two words of affirmation, however, he prays, "May our Lord, Jesus Christ himself, and God our Father . . . strengthen you" (2 Thess. 2:16–17). Just as he prays to both God the Father and Christ the exalted Lord, so he easily uses identical language for both the Father and the Son when mentioning the content of his prayer.

The Word of the Lord/God

The phrase "the word of God" occurs seven times in the Pauline corpus (1 Cor. 14:36; 2 Cor. 2:17; 4:2; Rom. 9:6; Col. 1:25; Titus 2:5; 2 Tim. 2:9), always with what is technically known as a subjective genitive, so that "God" is the grammatical subject of the "word" that has been spoken, either in Scripture (what we know as the Old Testament) or with reference to the gospel in some way. Whereas in some cases the nature of the genitive in the phrase "the word of the Lord" is less easy to determine—whether it is *about* the Lord (objective) or *from* the Lord (subjective)—in its first appearance in the corpus (1 Thess. 1:8), "of the Lord" is most likely objective. In other words, what is spreading rapidly is "the word about the Lord," referring to Christ.

This is likely also the case in its second occurrence, where Paul expresses desire for "the message of the Lord" to spread rapidly (2 Thess. 3:1). And there can be little question that, in its second appearance in his earlier letter, Paul is using "of the Lord" as a subjective genitive—that is, "the Lord" is the one who has spoken—in precisely the same way as with "the word of God": "According to the Lord's word, we tell you. . . ." (1 Thess. 4:15). This interchange is made certain by the follow-up of this phrase, which can refer only to Christ: "we who are still alive . . . until the coming of the Lord."

The Faithfulness of the Lord/God

One of the more consistent ways Yahweh is self-revealed in the Old Testament is in a primary attribute of *faithfulness*, meaning essentially that God can be completely trusted at all times and in all ways to be whom God has revealed himself to be. It is therefore not surprising that, in his first letter to the Thessalonians, Paul should appeal to such faithfulness with regard to God carrying out divine purposes in the lives of these believers: "The one who calls you [referring to God] is faithful" (1 Thess. 5:24). The Apostle then says in his next letter to them: "But the Lord is faithful" (2 Thess. 3:3). In the immediate context, where two sentences earlier Christ has been specifically identified as "the Lord" (2 Thess. 2:16–17), it is clear that Paul is referring to Christ as "the Lord." Thus even though elsewhere in his letters Paul speaks only of God's faithfulness (1 Cor. 1:9; 10:13; 2 Cor. 1:18), here he applies that language to Christ as well.

The Gospel of Our Lord/God

When reading Paul's letters one gets accustomed to the easy interchange between "the gospel of God" (1 Thess. 2:2, 8, 9), where the emphasis is on its *source*, and "the gospel of Christ" (1 Thess. 3:2), where the emphasis is on Christ as its basic *content*. However, in his second letter to these believers—in his long thanksgiving-turned-announcement of judgment against their persecutors with which the letter begins (2 Thess. 1:3–10)—Paul refers to the latter as "those who do not know God and do not obey *the gospel of our Lord, Jesus*" (v. 8). This unique moment in the New Testament is shaped to fit the immediate context, since this phrase is but one more adaptation of common language to fit the setting of Christ carrying out God's just judgment—in this case against those who are persecuting the Thessalonian believers. It is a remarkable adaptation of a common phrase, with the emphasis now on what the gospel has to do with the currently reigning Lord.

The Glory of the Lord/God

On several occasions in his letters Paul uses the phrase "the glory of God" as a way of speaking about the final goal of all things. The phrase is used to describe both the infinite greatness of God as such—for example, Paul's instructions to believers to do all things with God's glory in view (1 Cor. 10:31; Phil. 1:11)—and the sphere where God dwells (Rom. 5:2; Phil. 4:19). Paul uses both of these nuances of the phrase when speaking of Christ the Lord.

In Paul's second letter to the believers in Thessalonica, he asserts that the final goal of salvation is obtaining "the glory of our Lord, Jesus Christ" (2 Thess. 2:14)—that is, being together with him in the sphere of his glory. In his second letter to the Corinthian believers, he asserts that when believers turn to Christ by the Spirit they behold, or contemplate, "the *Lord's glory*" (2 Cor. 3:18; cf. 4:4). The immediate context in this case makes plain that the Lord's glory is that of Yahweh, glory that Moses had *not* been allowed to behold on Mount Sinai.

Paul Sent/Commissioned by Christ

In the Septuagint the Greek verb *apostellō* ("send") is regularly used for Yahweh's "sending," or "commissioning," messengers to the people who belong to God. This phenomenon explains why Paul can ask rhetorically, "How can anyone preach unless they are *sent*?" (Rom. 10:15), where he uses this verb, though without specifying the divine sender. But in an earlier letter when Paul speaks of his own ministry, he uses the same verb when he writes, "Christ did not *send* me to baptize, but to preach the gospel" (1 Cor. 1:17). To be sure, in this instance "Christ," not "the Lord," is the grammatical subject of the verb; nonetheless, Paul clearly considered this sending to be part of his experience, which he relates later in the letter when he asks rhetorically, "Have I not seen Jesus our Lord?" (9:1).

The Power of the Lord/God

One of the constants in the Old Testament understanding of God is that Yahweh is a God of great and unlimited power. Thus both creation and the redemption of Israel are regularly celebrated in the Psalter in terms of God's great love and power (e.g., Pss. 89:5–18; 145:3–13). Paul uses this same kind of language in his letters as well. For example, he celebrates God's power revealed in redemption and creation early on in his letter to the believers in Rome: "the gospel . . . is the power of God. . . . For since the creation of the world God's invisible qualities—his eternal power and divine nature—have been clearly seen, being understood from what has been made" (Rom. 1:16, 20).

Paul uses similar language with regard to the person and work of Christ. In the second matter he addresses in his first letter to the believers in Corinth—the difficult situation of the incestuous man (1 Cor. 5)—Paul begins by urging them in the context of the gathered assembly, when "the *power* of our Lord, Jesus, is present" (v. 4), to carry out the judgment that he has pronounced "in the name of our Lord, Jesus" (v. 3). Although "power" in this case is very likely an oblique reference to the Spirit, it is of christological import that God's Spirit and power are understood to be present as the power of the exalted Lord, Jesus. Similarly, in his next letter to the Corinthian believers Paul reports Christ's answer to his prayer concerning his "thorn in [the] flesh" (2 Cor. 12:7) that *"my power* is made perfect in weakness" (v. 9; cf. 1 Cor. 1:22–25). Thus Paul goes on to affirm that he would gladly bear such weaknesses "so that *Christ's power* may rest on [him]" (2 Cor. 12:9).

The Lord/God Has Given

In the narrative of Israel's creation of the tabernacle (Exod. 31:2–5; 36:1–2) we are told (in the Septuagint) that "God gave to [Bezalel]" the wisdom and skill for the task (36:1). In Paul's second letter to the Corinthians he uses this same language to refer to his own gifting for apostolic ministry: "*God . . . through Christ . . . gave us* the ministry of reconciliation" (2 Cor. 5:18). But in his earlier letter to them, Paul refers to his own and Apollos's gifting as coming from the Lord: "as *the Lord* has given to each" (1 Cor. 3:5, my trans.).

The Lord/God Wills

Paul begins his first letter to the Corinthians by noting that his apostleship is "by the will of God" (1 Cor. 1:1), a phrase that occurs some thirteen times in his letters. But in two remarkable moments in this same letter, Paul speaks of returning to Corinth "if *the Lord* is willing" (4:19) and "if *the Lord* permits" (16:7), thus seamlessly transferring this absolute prerogative of God to Christ the Lord.

Pleasing the Lord/God

In Paul's discussion of what he perceives to be the advantages of singleness over marriage, he asserts that a single person is able to devote all of his or her energy to a single thing: how to "please *the Lord*" (1 Cor. 7:32). In most other such moments in his letters—both earlier (1 Thess. 2:15; 4:1) and later (e.g., Rom. 8:8; 12:1–2; 14:18; Phil. 4:18)—Paul speaks of "pleasing *God*." Here is yet another Old Testament way of speaking (e.g., Ps. 19:14; Prov. 16:7) that has been taken over by Paul and directly applied to the Lord, Christ (cf. 2 Cor. 5:8–9).

The Assembly(ies) of Christ/God

In what is less a divine prerogative and more a matter of divine possession, Paul regularly refers to the believing communities with the term *ekklēsia*, a happy choice of terms since it does double duty: (1) it picks up the language for the local "assembly" of people in the Greek city-states, which (2) had been conveniently used by the Septuagint translators to speak of the gathered "congregation" of Israel. Paul's genitive descriptor (used as a possessive) for this "assembly" is ordinarily "the assembly [or assemblies] *of God*," but in signing off his letter to the believers in Rome he just as easily refers to the churches who are sending greetings to Rome as "the assemblies *of Christ*" (Rom. 16:16, my trans.).

The Fear of the Lord/LORD

The penultimate example of this kind of interchange between "God" and "the Lord" is one of the truly significant moments in the corpus. It is a sure indicator of the ease with which Paul transfers divine prerogatives and attributes to Christ and thus of Paul's understanding of Christ as fully divine and as one who can regularly stand in a role that is biblically otherwise assigned to God alone. Although the phrase "the fear of the LORD" occurs most often in the Wisdom literature, it is basic to Israel's understanding of Yahweh and of their relationship to the eternal One. Here the word "fear" seldom, if ever, carries its ordinary meaning in English, as having to do with being frightened. Rather, in almost every case it is a term denoting reverential awe, which is described in the Old Testament as "the beginning of wisdom" (Prov. 9:10).

Significantly, in a passage where Paul puts emphasis on Christ the Lord as the eschatological judge of his people (2 Cor. 5:10), he follows up by referring to knowing "what it is to *fear the Lord*," by which he undoubtedly means Christ (v. 11). As with the usage of this phrase in Wisdom literature, here it refers not to their being fearful of Christ but to their being in reverential awe of him.

The Spirit of the Lord/God

This rehearsal of divine prerogatives shared by God and Christ the Lord is now brought to conclusion with the only one that does not occur in the first four of Paul's preserved letters: that the one Holy Spirit, who is most often referred to as "the Spirit of God," is on three occasions specifically identified by Paul as "the Spirit of Christ." We will discuss this phenomenon in further detail in the concluding chapter, but here we make a few initial observations

When moving toward his instructions about the role of the Spirit in his letter to the Galatians, Paul stipulates that God "sent *the Spirit of his Son* into our hearts" (Gal. 4:6), who elicits the *Abba*-cry. Similarly, in his later letter to the believers in Rome this interchange is specific and thoroughgoing. What identifies the believer as one who does not live "in the realm of the flesh" is that *"the Spirit of God* lives in you"* (Rom. 8:9). But then Paul immediately makes the interchange: "And if anyone does not have *the Spirit of Christ*, they do not belong to Christ."

Since for Paul there is also only "one Spirit" (Eph. 4:4; cf. 1 Cor. 12:4), this kind of interchange is a crowning expression of Paul's understanding of the full deity of Christ. Along with other moments in his letters we have discussed, it serves as the basis for his triadic understanding of God that—along with the Gospel of John and Hebrews—eventually led the church to express this understanding in trinitarian terms. However one is finally to articulate the *relationship* between the one God and the one Lord, this kind of thing can be said by Paul only because he believes that the incarnate Son and now exalted Lord was eternally preexistent and fully equal with the Father. And this reality is what leads us to our concluding chapter. But before that we need to sum up the preceding discussion.

Conclusion

The evidence of this chapter puts the capstone on the high Christology in Paul that we have regularly observed in the preceding chapters. And it does so by way of the rich possibilities for Paul of the "title" for Jesus that had found expression in the earliest Aramaic-speaking communities, the confession that Jesus is "the Lord." It is probably not accidental, therefore, that in its three appearances in Paul's letters this confession always occurs in the order "the Lord is Jesus [Christ]" (1 Cor. 12:3; Rom. 10:9; Phil. 2:11; my trans.). Indeed, even though it was the earthly, incarnate Jesus who was raised from the dead, it was at Christ's exaltation that God the Father bestowed on the preexistent Son the divine name of "the Lord" itself.

It was through the happy circumstance that the divine name had been translated in the Septuagint by way of the Aramaic *Adonai* ("the LORD" = Yahweh) that Paul was able to have it both ways. The preexistent Son, who became incarnate as Jesus of Nazareth, received the "name" at his vindication. But at the same time, by using *ho Kyrios* ("the Lord") exclusively to refer to the risen Christ, the Apostle could include the Son in the divine identity in a complete way, but without absolute identification (merging the two into one) and without the Son usurping the role of God the Father.

Given the evidence that has been rehearsed in this chapter, we emphasize by way of conclusion two matters. First, one can hardly miss the rich variety of ways Paul has included Christ in the divine identity by means of the name-turned-title, *ho Kyrios* ("the Lord"). This phenomenon occurs repeatedly in the earliest letters in the corpus and is maintained throughout, all the way to his last letter, 2 Timothy. This phenomenon happens regularly in two ways: first, full sentences or paragraphs that refer to Yahweh and, second, in all sorts of shorter phrases that in the Old Testament are primarily the exclusive province of Yahweh but that in Paul's writing, by means of the Septuagint, are regularly attributed to the exalted Lord, Jesus Christ.

Second, as we have noted repeatedly throughout the book, one can scarcely miss out on how theologically unselfconsciously and nearly offhandedly Paul transfers titles and prerogatives from Yahweh to Christ. Here is a man not trying to assert anything unusual about the role of the presently exalted Lord but who simply assumes it in every way in the process of dealing with all kinds of other matters in his churches. Perhaps even more significant is that he equally assumed that this understanding was shared by his readers, especially since this issue is never directly raised or responded to as such in any of his letters. This is clearly a matter of common ground between Paul and his letter recipients, on the basis of which he argues all kinds of other matters. But all throughout, his appropriation of Old Testament Yahweh language to refer to the divine activity of the reigning Lord, Jesus, has inherent in it an understanding of Christ as assuming roles that traditionally, and exclusively, belong to God alone.

Thus we conclude from the evidence that Paul offers as high a Christology as one could imagine. It is therefore not a matter of wonder that when the apostle John some years later chose to write a more reflective rendition of Christ's incarnation and life of ministry, this way of understanding who Jesus was is expressed so boldly from the outset (John 1:1–18) and serves as the assumed common ground between him and his readers. As we will see in the concluding chapter, the early believers were *practicing* trinitarians, even if the necessary articulation of the trinitarian doctrine would come later, when the assumed realities expressed by all the writers of the documents that became our New Testament would need further articulation and clarification in the larger Roman world. By then the assumptions held in common at an earlier time would need elaboration and explanation for a gentile world not accustomed to the biblical framework of the writers and readers of these first-generation documents. And so the letters of Paul, along with the Gospel of John and Hebrews, were brought into the conversation to give expression to the trinitarian understanding of the one and only God. For whatever else was true for Paul, he was an absolutely thoroughgoing monotheist from start to finish. What is new is his devotion to Christ and his resulting way of speaking about Christ.

Conclusion

Paul as a Proto-trinitarian

Even the most casual reading of the preceding chapters would force on one the theological necessity of trying to come to terms with the twofold reality of Paul's high Christology—his view of Christ as the preexistent Son and the exalted one who is given the "name" Lord—combined with his vigorously held monotheism. Consistent with the Jewish tradition in which he had been raised, Paul regularly asserts that there is only *one* God. So we ask in this concluding chapter: What does it mean for an avid monotheist to envision the one Deity as Father and Son? Yet there is more: in the preceding chapter we noted the *role* of the Spirit in Paul's understanding of Christ as well as Paul's understanding of the Spirit's *relationship* to the Son and the Father. Our goal in this conclusion, therefore, is to carefully examine the data to demonstrate that it was not just John's Gospel but equally Paul's thirteen letters that caused the church in time to express itself in trinitarian, not binitarian, terms. In this concluding chapter, therefore, several theological matters will be examined, not with a solution in view but simply to raise awareness and offer some brief discussion of the issues.

The first aim of this conclusion, therefore, is to point out the considerable christological implications found in Paul's many and varied statements that conjoin the Spirit with Christ (and the Father) in the economy of salvation. That is, we ask what the christological implications are of Paul's understanding of the relationship of Christ and the Spirit, as much as that can be discovered in his various, not intentionally theological, statements. At the same time our interest here is in examining where Paul fits into a trajectory that caused these early, thoroughgoing monotheists to speak of Christ and the Spirit and their relationship to God the Father in such a way that finally resulted in the fully developed trinitarian resolution of the fourth and fifth centuries.

As a way to engage these matters we need first to look briefly at Paul's basic understanding of the person and role of the Spirit in the divine economy.[1] That will be followed by a brief look at Paul's understanding of Christ's relationship with the Spirit, as that emerges almost incidentally in the Pauline corpus. All of this together points to an especially high Christology in Paul, while at the same time pushing us toward a latent triadic understanding of the one God. This in turn suggests that Paul held to a kind of proto-trinitarian view of God, even though the Apostle himself never comes close to explaining how a strict monotheist could talk about God in this triadic way—especially in what might seem to be so casual a manner.

The Person and Role of the Spirit in Paul's Thought

We begin our discussion of the Spirit with a brief overview of Paul's use of the word *pneuma* as a referent to the Holy Spirit, which occurs approximately 120 times in the Pauline corpus. Of these the most common referent is simply to "the Spirit," while seventeen times the more fulsome name, "the Holy Spirit," appears. But on twelve occasions Paul speaks of the Spirit as "the Spirit of God," which from the larger perspective of the whole of Scripture should come as no surprise. Most significant to our present study, however, are the four times Paul refers to the same Holy Spirit as "the Spirit of the Lord" (2 Cor. 3:17); "the Spirit of [God's] Son" (Gal. 4:6); "the Spirit of Christ" (Rom. 8:9); and "the Spirit of Jesus Christ" (Phil. 1:19). Before examining these passages, several matters

---

1. For a fuller discussion of these matters, see my books *God's Empowering Presence: The Holy Spirit in the Letters of Paul* (Grand Rapids: Baker Academic, 2011 [Peabody, MA: Hendrickson, 1994]) and *Paul, the Spirit, and the People of God* (Grand Rapids: Baker Academic, 2011 [Peabody, MA: Hendrickson, 1996]).

about Paul's understanding of the Spirit need to be highlighted, since many believers share the sentiments of a former student who once declared in exasperation: "God the Father, I know; God the Son, I love; but the Holy Spirit is a gray, oblong blur!"—something I still remember after several decades because it gave voice to what has been true for a great many believers.

Although Paul clearly understood the Spirit to be intimately related both to God the Father and to Christ, he also understood the Spirit to have a distinct personhood in his own right, as we can see in the many texts where the Spirit is the subject of actions that belong to personhood (given in their assumed chronological order):

The Spirit searches all things (1 Cor. 2:10).

The Spirit knows the mind of God (1 Cor. 2:11).

The Spirit teaches the content of the gospel to believers (1 Cor. 2:13).

The Spirit dwells among/within believers (1 Cor. 3:16; cf. Rom. 8:11; 2 Tim. 1:14).

The Spirit accomplishes all things (1 Cor. 12:11).

The Spirit gives life to those who believe (2 Cor. 3:6).

The Spirit cries out from within our hearts (Gal. 4:6).

The Spirit has desires that are in opposition to the flesh (Gal. 5:17).

The Spirit leads us in the ways of God (Gal. 5:18; Rom. 8:14).

The Spirit bears witness with our own spirits (Rom. 8:16).

The Spirit helps us in our weakness (Rom. 8:26).

The Spirit intercedes on our behalf (Rom. 8:26–27).

The Spirit works all things together for our ultimate good (Rom. 8:28).

The Spirit strengthens believers (Eph. 3:16).

The Spirit is grieved by our sinfulness (Eph. 4:30).

Furthermore, in Paul's list of some of the *fruit* of the Spirit's indwelling believers (Gal. 5:22–23), he gives expression to the personal attributes of God in their adjectival form, some of which occur above as verbs. In addition, there are three moments in Paul's letters where he makes clear that he not only understood the Spirit as person but that he also understood the Spirit as in some sense distinct from the Father and the Son.

First, in his long exposition of the role of the Spirit in the life of the believer in his letter to "all in Rome who are loved by God and called to be God's holy people" (Rom. 1:7), Paul asserts that it is the Spirit who gives us "adoption to sonship,"[2] as attested by the Spirit's prompting within us of the *Abba*-cry (8:15). The Spirit becomes the *second* necessary witness to our adoption, thus reflecting Paul's biblical heritage that everything shall be established by two or three witnesses (Deut. 19:15; cf. 2 Cor. 13:1). Whatever else, this is the language of *personhood*, not that of some kind of impersonal influence or power. One need only look at the Apostle's brief argument with the Corinthians as to the nature of true wisdom (1 Cor. 2:6–16), where he uses the analogy of human interior consciousness (only one's own spirit knows one's mind) to insist that the Spirit alone knows the mind of God. There Paul writes, "The Spirit searches all things, even the deep things of God" (v. 10). And because of this singular relationship with God, the Spirit alone knows and reveals God's otherwise hidden wisdom (v. 7).

Second, the various triadic passages in Paul's writings speak strongly against the conflation of the risen Christ and the Spirit who is poured out on believers. The two primary texts that have been used to argue for such conflation are the result of Paul using moments from the Septuagint to further other concerns (2 Cor. 3:17; 1 Cor. 15:45). But Paul has no intention of identifying the risen Christ with the Spirit. The same is true with the crucial passage in Romans, which we discuss at some length below, where Paul follows the phrase "the *Spirit* of Christ" with the phrase "if Christ is in you" (8:9–11). In context this can mean only "if Christ by his Spirit is in you," and thus has nothing to do with conflating the Spirit with Christ. Rather, for Paul the Spirit has personhood in his own right. Even though he is intimately related to both the Father and the Son, the Spirit is also quite clearly distinct from them. This is made plain especially by the many triadic statements in Paul where the roles (noted below) of the Father, the Son, and the Spirit in our salvation are distinct and unique—even though everything is seen ultimately to come from the one God.

2. Here, as elsewhere, "sonship" clearly includes men and women alike as God's children.

Third, Paul's triadic way of speaking about our human salvation will not allow us to confuse or conflate either the person or the work of the Son with that of the Spirit. In Paul's worldview, "between the times" as it were, *the Son* is now seated "at [God's] right hand in the heavenly realms" (Eph. 1:20), where he currently makes intercession for us (Rom. 8:34). Significantly, just a couple of sentences earlier in this letter Paul refers to *the Spirit* indwelling us and helping us in our times of weakness by interceding from within, speaking for us what is inexpressible (8:26), which God knows because God "knows the mind of the Spirit" (v. 27). Thus to put it in different terms, in the present "geography" of heaven and earth, both Father and Son are seen as dwelling in heaven, while the Spirit is seen as (in)dwelling on earth.

It is thus certain that Paul understood the Spirit both as personal and as distinct from the Father and the Son—to borrow language of the later creeds—although intimately related to both as God's and Christ's own personal presence within and among us, carrying on the ministry of Christ in the present age.

Christ and the Spirit in Paul's Thought

Just as the coming of the Son has forever marked our understanding of God, who is henceforth known as "the Father of our Lord, Jesus Christ," likewise the coming of Christ has forever marked our understanding of the Spirit. Whatever else, the Spirit of God is also the Spirit of Christ (2 Cor. 3:17; Gal. 4:6; Rom. 8:9; Phil. 1:19), who carries on the work of Christ following his resurrection and subsequent assumption to the place of authority at God's right hand. To have received the Spirit of God (1 Cor. 2:12) is to have access to the mind of Christ (v. 16)—to understand what Christ is all about in bringing us salvation.

For Paul, therefore, Christ provides a fuller definition to the Spirit: people of the Spirit are God's *children*, fellow *heirs* with God's Son (Rom. 8:14–17). At the same time, Christ is the absolute criterion for what is truly Spirit activity (e.g., 1 Cor. 12:3). Indeed, the Apostle says, to have the Spirit of Christ indwelling us means that Christ himself is present with us (Rom. 8:9–10). It is fair to say that Paul's doctrine of the Spirit is Christ-centered in the sense that Christ and his work help to define both the person of the Spirit and the Spirit's active involvement in the ongoing life of the believer.

For the most part the relationship between the *role* of Christ and the Spirit in the new covenant era is fairly straightforward. This comes out most often in the many instances where Paul speaks of the believers' salvation in triadic terms in affirmations or assertions that occur throughout the corpus of letters both early and late. These include his semicreedal passages where he is affirming our salvation:

> But we ought always to thank God for you, brothers and sisters loved by the Lord, because *God* chose you as firstfruits to be saved through the sanctifying work of *the Spirit.* . . . . He called you to this through our gospel, that you might share in the glory of *our Lord, Jesus Christ.* (2 Thess. 2:13–14)

> You were justified [= God justified you] in the name of the *Lord, Jesus Christ,* and *by the Spirit of our God.* (1 Cor. 6:11; cf. 2 Cor. 1:21–22; Gal. 4:4–7; Rom. 8:3–4, 15–17; Titus 3:4–7)

The relationship between the Spirit and Christ is also expressed in many other seemingly offhanded moments, soteriological or otherwise:

> Before your very eyes *Jesus Christ* was clearly portrayed as crucified. . . . So again I ask, does *God* give you *his Spirit* and work miracles among you by the works of the law . . . ? (Gal. 3:1, 5)

> I know that through your prayers and God's provision of *the Spirit of Jesus Christ* what has happened to me will turn out for my deliverance. . . . For it is we who are the circumcision, we who serve *God* by *his Spirit,* who boast in *Christ Jesus.* (Phil. 1:19; 3:3; cf. 1 Cor. 1:4–7; 2:4–5, 12; 6:19–20; 2 Cor. 3:16–18; Rom. 5:5–8; 8:9–11; 15:16, 18–19, 30; Col. 3:16; Eph. 1:3, 17–20; 2:17–18, 19–22; 3:16–19; 5:18–19)

Our point here is that, for Paul, human redemption is the combined activity of the Father, Son, and Spirit. Thus his grammar of salvation is quite consistent, even though it is usually quite ad hoc and thus expressed in a variety of ways. For Paul, salvation is (1) predicated on the love of God, which sets it in motion; (2) effected in history through the death and resurrection of Christ the Son; and (3) actualized in the life of believers through the power of the Holy Spirit. Although Paul gives expression to this reality in any number of ways, a passage in his letter to the believers in Rome offers a typical example: the love of God that found expression historically in Christ's dying for us (Rom. 5:8) is what the Holy Spirit has poured out in our hearts (v. 5).

Thus in one of the most revealing of these moments in his impassioned letter to the believers in Galatia, Paul speaks in identical terms, first of God having "sent his Son" (Gal. 4:4) and then of God having "sent the Spirit of his Son into our hearts" (v. 6). In the first instance the sending was for the purpose of effecting salvation in the course of human history: Jesus was sent by the Father into human history ("born of a woman") in the context of historic Judaism ("born under the law") for the express purpose of human redemption. This first sending concluded with the Son's resurrection and exaltation, the latter being assumed in a variety of ways throughout the letter. So the second sending, that of "the Spirit of the Son," occurred postascension, and from Paul's point of view occurred precisely to put into effect the life that Christ had secured for us by his death. This presence of the Son by means of the Spirit of the Son is what actualizes our own "sonship," that is, our adoption as God's children—based on the redemptive work of the Son and actualized in believers' lives by the indwelling of the Spirit of the Son.

The net result of all of this is that in his incarnation the Son of God came into human history, bearing the divine image and thus the divine presence on earth. What *the Son* came to effect was the restoration of the divine image in those who would become God's children through faith in him; what *the Spirit of the Son* came to effect was the actual re-creating of that image in those who through Christ and the Spirit are themselves the *children of God*. And what is at stake here is not one's personal life as such but our communal life together as one people of God.

These various data push us in two directions theologically. First, as already noted, there is in Paul's view a clear distinction between the risen Christ and the Holy Spirit whom God the Father sent into the world. Indeed, the narrowly focused data presented in the preceding chapters could perhaps be seen as part of a larger New Testament picture, where God's activity in our redemption is expressed basically in terms of the

Father and the Son. But in Paul that is not the whole picture. In the end it is the triadic *experience* of God and of God's effecting our salvation, the so-called economic Trinity, that led the later church to express this divine triad in terms of the ontological Trinity, God's very *being* understood as Father, Son, and Holy Spirit together as one God.

Second, what is striking for Pauline Christology is the ease with which the Apostle, when speaking of the Spirit, can shift language between the Father and the Son. Nowhere does this happen in a more telling way than toward the outset of Romans 8, where the Spirit not only *actualizes* the work of Christ in the believer's life but also *enables* the believer to live and behave in such a way as to bring glory to God, both Father and Son. Thus, near the beginning of this remarkable presentation of life in the Spirit (vv. 9–10), the presently indwelling Spirit is spoken of in successive clauses in a most casual, offhanded manner as the way both the Father and the Son, who dwell in heaven, are seen to be present on earth, now dwelling in the heart of the believer: "You, however, are not in the realm of the flesh but are in the realm of the Spirit, if indeed *the Spirit of God* lives in you. And if anyone does not have *the Spirit of Christ*, they do not belong to Christ" (v. 9). To be a genuine New Testament Christian is to be genuinely trinitarian.

Indeed, if the data of our preceding chapters do not themselves definitively bear out Paul's view of Christ as fully divine, then surely the ease with which Paul here refers to the Spirit should do so. In the space of two clauses, where the second is obviously picking up what was said in the first, the *one Spirit* (cf. 1 Cor. 12:4; Eph. 4:4) is expressed by Paul first as "the Spirit of God [who] lives in you" and then immediately as "the Spirit of Christ" (Rom 8:9). Since for Paul there are not two Spirits, nor is there more than one God, such sentences as these are what almost demand some kind of theological and christological resolution on our part—not in the sense of our finding out God, as it were, but of our trying to comprehend, or put language to, the ultimately incomprehensible divine reality: one God in three distinct persons. Thus rather than thinking of Paul as either confused or confusing by what he affirms with these words, we can recognize that it is the role of the Spirit—as simultaneously the Spirit of God and the Spirit of Christ—to both emphasize the full deity of Christ and cause us in the end to think of the one God in triadic terms.

Paul and the Divine Triad

One of the more interesting phenomena regarding Paul's letters, given that he writes mostly to gentile converts who would have been primarily polytheistic, is how seldom he puts any emphasis on the basic Jewish theological reality that there is but "one God." The actual language occurs in only six passages (1 Cor. 8:4, 6; Gal. 3:20; Rom. 3:30; Eph. 4:6; 1 Tim. 2:5); is implied in yet another (1 Cor. 12:6), where "the same" means "one and the same," as a follow-up sentence makes clear about the Spirit: v. 11); and is expressed once in terms of "the *only* God" (1 Tim. 1:17). Since this is so presuppositional for Paul and assumed to be true for his readers, the need seldom arises for him to make a point of it.

But in five of the seven occurrences of this term or concept, Paul's affirmation of his consistent monotheism occurs in conjunction with equal emphasis on either Christ (1 Cor. 8:6; Gal. 3:20; 1 Tim. 2:5) or on Christ *and* the Spirit (1 Cor. 12:6; Eph. 4:6). Three of these passages (1 Cor. 8:6; 12:6; Eph. 4:6) call for special attention because, even though in each case the work of the divine dyad or triad is expressed, the emphasis in each case is on the reality of the *oneness* of God in the context of emphasis on the oneness of Christ and the oneness of the Spirit (if mentioned).

Along with more than twenty passages where the divine three are mentioned in their roles in regard to human redemption,[3] the present passages are constant reminders that Paul's experience of Christ and the Spirit caused him to think of the one God in terms that included the Son and the Spirit. We have had reason above to look carefully at the most important of the dyadic passages, where Paul deliberately expanded the Jewish Shema to affirm the Father as the "one God" and to include Christ the Son as "the one Lord" (1 Cor. 8:6). Here we briefly unpack the significance of three triadic passages for Pauline Christology.

1 CORINTHIANS 12:4–6

There are different kinds of gifts, but the same Spirit distributes them. There are different kinds of service, but the same Lord. There are different

---

3. In *God's Empowering Presence*, I refer to this as "soteriological Trinitarianism" and include a summarizing list of these passages (841–42).

kinds of working, but in all of them and in everyone it is the same God at work.

At the beginning of Paul's long correction and instruction regarding Spirit manifestations in the gathered community (1 Cor. 12–14), some proto-trinitarian implications appear. Paul's aim throughout the passage is to broaden the Corinthian believers' perspective on the activity of the Spirit in their gatherings for worship (over against their apparently singular interest in speaking in tongues). His way of doing it could be considered as something of an overkill, since in this lengthy argument he offers no less than seven different listings of Spirit manifestations, no two of which are alike! However, in each case the problem child, the gift of speaking in tongues, appears either at the beginning or the end of the list. It is because of the uniqueness of the situation that the divine triad appears in this case in the order of "Spirit . . . Lord . . . God" (12:4–6), the only one of its kind in all of his preserved letters.

Thus he begins the entire discussion by noting that *diversity reflects the nature of God* and is therefore the true evidence of the work of the one God in their midst. The divine triad is presuppositional to the entire argument, and these opening foundational words are the more telling precisely because they are so unstudied and so freely and unselfconsciously expressed. Just as there is only one God, from whom and for whom are all things, and one Lord, through whom all things came (1 Cor. 8:6), so there is only one Spirit (12:9), through whose agency the one God is manifest among them in a variety of ways in the believing community.

2 CORINTHIANS 13:14

May the grace of our Lord, Jesus Christ, and the love of God, and the fellowship of the Holy Spirit be with you all.

The remarkable grace-benediction at the end of Paul's second letter to the Corinthian believers offers all kinds of theological keys to Paul's understanding of salvation as well as of the eternal God. Several unique features make this passage particularly important for understanding Paul. First is that the benediction is composed and intended for the occasion and thus functions precisely as do all of his other grace-benedictions, which all begin exactly this way, with "the grace of our Lord, Jesus Christ." This is what determines the unusual order of Christ, God, and the Spirit.

Second, this benediction summarizes the core elements of Paul's unique passion: the gospel, with its focus on salvation in Christ, which is equally available by faith to gentile and Jew alike. That the *love of God* is the foundation of Paul's view of salvation is stated with passion and clarity in several moments elsewhere in the corpus of letters (e.g., Rom. 5:1–11; 8:31–39; Eph. 1:3–14). The *grace of our Lord, Jesus Christ,* is what gave concrete expression to that love; through Christ's suffering and death on behalf of his loved ones, God accomplished salvation for them at one moment in human history. The *participation in the Holy Spirit* continually actualizes that love and grace in the life of the believer and the believing community. Indeed, this is precisely how the living God not only brings people into an intimate and abiding relationship with God, as the God of all grace, but also causes them to participate in all the benefits of that grace and salvation—that is, by indwelling them in the present with God's own presence and thus guaranteeing their final eschatological glory.

Third, this benediction serves as our entrée into Paul's understanding of God as such, which had been so radically affected for him by the twin realities of the death and resurrection of Christ and the gift of the Spirit. Granted, Paul does not here *assert* the deity of Christ and the Spirit. What he does is more telling by far: he *equates the activity of the three divine persons* (to use the language of the creeds) in concert and in one prayer, with the clause about God the Father standing in second place! This suggests that Paul was at least proto-trinitarian. According to his benediction, the believer knows and experiences the one God as Father, Son, and Spirit, and when dealing with Christ and the Spirit one is dealing with God every bit as much as when dealing with the Father.

Thus, while making a fundamental distinction between God, Christ, and Spirit, this benediction also expresses in shorthand form what is found throughout Paul's letters—namely, that salvation is the cooperative work of the Father, the Son, and the Spirit.

Ephesians 4:4–6

There is one body and one Spirit, just as you were called to one hope when you were called; one Lord, one faith, one baptism; one God and Father of all, who is over all and through all and in all.

In his letter to the believers in Ephesus, written some years after his Corinthian correspondence, one finds the same combination as in Paul's second letter to the Corinthians (2 Cor. 13:14)—a *creedal* formulation expressed in terms of the distinguishable activities of the triune God (Eph. 4:4–6). The basis for Christian unity is the one and only God, who has been revealed through both the incarnation and the subsequent gift of the Spirit as Father, Son, and Holy Spirit. Thus the church as one body is the work of the *one Spirit* (cf. 1 Cor. 12:13), by whom also we live our present eschatological existence in *one hope*, since the Spirit is the "down payment on our inheritance" (Eph. 1:13–14, my trans.). All of this has been made possible for us by our *one Lord*, in whom all have *one faith* and to which faith all have given witness through their *one baptism*. The source of all of these realities is the *one and only God* "who is over all and through all and in all" (Eph. 4:6). Again, because at issue is the work of the Spirit, "the unity of the Spirit" (v. 3), the order is the same as in 1 Corinthians 12:4–6 (Spirit, Lord, God), which works from the present, experienced reality to the foundational reality of the one God.

If the last phrase in this passage reemphasizes the unity of the one God, who is ultimately responsible for all things—past, present, and future—and subsumes the work of the Spirit and the Son under that of God the Father, the entire passage at the same time puts into creedal form the affirmation that God is *experienced* as a triune reality. Precisely on the basis of such experience and language the later church maintained its biblical integrity by expressing all of this in explicitly trinitarian language. And Paul's formulations, which include the work of both Christ and the Spirit, form part of the basis for these creedal expressions.

In this passage (Eph. 4:4–6), as in 1 Corinthians 12:4–6, discussed above, Paul is emphasizing rather than abandoning the basic theological reality of his tradition: that there is only one God and that the one God is God alone. But this emphasis occurs primarily in contexts where he is deliberately expanding the identity of the one God to include the "one Lord" and the "one Spirit." And it is the recognition of this reality that led the early church to wrestle with the biblical data so profoundly.

Conclusion

As we end this study, we note that even though some Christians feel uncomfortable with the Nicene "settlement," which spoke of Christ as being of one "substance," or "being," with the Father, it is not difficult to see how such language was the natural result of trying to come to terms with the biblical revelation as it existed on predominantly Greek soil. What seems to be certain from the Pauline data is the inevitability of speaking of God at least in terms of the economic Trinity: God revealed to us as Father, Son, and Spirit in the work of our salvation.

Anything less than this twofold affirmation would seem to be the result of our own modern presuppositions and limited human reasoning rather than learning from God's own self-revelation as Father, Son, and Holy Spirit. So it is ours to let God be God and to regularly fall on our faces, as it were, and worship with praise and thanksgiving the eternal One who should so care for the likes of us fallen ones. And so I conclude by offering thanks to God in my historical denominational way: *Hallelujah! Eternal praises be to the one and only God!*

> For us there is but one God, the Father, from whom all things came and for whom we live, and there is but one Lord, Jesus Christ, through whom all things came and through whom we live. (1 Cor. 8:6)

> For you know the grace of our Lord, Jesus Christ, that though he was rich, yet for your sake he became poor, so that you through his poverty might become rich. (2 Cor. 8:9)

> But when the set time had fully come, God sent his Son, born of a woman, born under the law, to redeem those under the law, that we might receive adoption to sonship. (Gal. 4:4)

> For what the law was powerless to do because it was weakened by the flesh, God did by sending his own Son in the likeness of sinful flesh to be a sin offering. (Rom. 8:3)

For in Christ all the fullness of the Deity lives in bodily form. (Col. 2:9)

Who, being in very nature God, did not consider equality with God something to be used to his own advantage; rather, he made himself nothing by taking the very nature of a servant, being made in human likeness. And being found in appearance as a man, he humbled himself by becoming obedient to death—even death on a cross. (Phil. 2:6–8)

Here is a trustworthy saying that deserves full acceptance: Christ Jesus came into the world to save sinners. (1 Tim. 1:15)

This grace was given us in Christ Jesus before the beginning of time, but it has now been revealed through the appearing of our Savior, Christ Jesus, who has destroyed death and brought life and immortality to light through the gospel. (2 Tim. 1:9–10)

Glossary

amanuensis. The person who pens a document, who in Paul's case would most often be taking it by dictation (see, e.g., Rom. 16:22).

Aramaic. The language spoken by Palestinian Jews in the first century, and thus the native tongue of Jesus.

assize. A court trial.

benedictory prayer. A form of prayer that is spoken indirectly to God on behalf of believers in Christ.

catena. A collection, or connected series, of similar items.

CE. Short for the Common Era, the contemporary way of saying AD (*Ante Domini*, the year of our Lord).

Christology. The doctrine of the person of Christ—who he was and is and the meaning of his life and work.

cruciform. A life patterned after Jesus's, which led to his crucifixion—that is, a life lived so as to benefit others without considering the cost.

Docetism. An early heresy that asserted Christ's humanity to be only apparent, not real.

ecclesiology. The doctrine of the church (derived from Greek *ekklēsia*, meaning "assembly").

election. The doctrine of God's choice in the salvation of those who have become believers.

eschatology. The doctrine of the end times (derived from Greek *eschatos*, meaning "last").

the fall. The sin of Adam and Eve, which led to the pervasive nature of sin in the entire human race.

imago Dei. Latin for "the image of God," describing Christ as fully bearing the divine image in his incarnation.

incarnation. The doctrine of Christ becoming human.

inclusio. A (usually) deliberate arrangement of words, sentences, or ideas in an ABBA pattern (e.g., "she said . . . said she").

intertextuality. The apparently conscious use by a New Testament author of the language from a known Old Testament passage in a new context for Christian believers.

justification. An understanding of salvation from the perspective of being released from the bondage of the law.

the Lord's table. Paul's own language for what came to called the Eucharist, the thanksgiving meal, or communion.

Messiah. The Hebrew's hoped-for, longed-for divine deliverer.

189

prayer-wish. A written prayer that indirectly expresses prayer to God with the recipients in view and for their sake.

presupposition. A background belief that is assumed rather than argued for, which often serves as the foundation for other beliefs or arguments.

progeny. A specific set of heirs of a given family line.

Psalter. The Old Testament book of Psalms.

redeemer. One who purchases someone else so as to set him or her free, as from slavery.

redemption. The act of purchasing someone so as to set him or her free, as from slavery.

soteriology. The doctrine of salvation (derived from Greek *sōtērion*, meaning "salvation").

suzerain. A ruler or sovereign.

triadic. An adjective used in reference to the divine Trinity.

Subject Index

Scripture Index